SELF-ADAPTIVE OPTIONS & CURRENCY TRADING

FOR THE

VOLATILE MARKETS OF THE 21ST CENTURY

by

JON SCHILLER, PHD

Including
OEX Index Options
High Volume Common Stock Options
Commodity Futures Options
Currency Trading Using Market Triggers
Financial Neural Networks

PublishAmerica
Baltimore

Options and Currency trading is risky and is not suited for everyone. The information in this book is believed to be accurate, but the author and publisher cannot guarantee the strategies described will not suffer losses.

First printing

ISBN: 1-4137-5963-7
PUBLISHED BY PUBLISHAMERICA, LLLP
www.publishamerica.com
Baltimore

Printed in the United States of America

Table of Contents

Appendices

Foreword

The main thrust of this book is to show you how, with inexpensive tools, you can begin with a limited amount of capital and make your capital grow impressively. You can easily double your capital annually. I have examined the Index Options available for trading and have selected the best for reasons discussed in the following pages. Also, I have sifted through a number of common stock options and selected the best stock options to trade.

In response to the interests of readers of my previous two options books (*The 100% Return Options Trading Strategy* and *The Insiders Automatic Options Strategy* published by Windsor Books), I have selected the best Commodity Futures Options to trade and I describe the strategies in this book. I describe how the Welles-Wilder Indicator, whose equations are included, can be used to decide when to open Index Options, Stock Options, and Future Options positions and make a short-term profit.

Finally I learned from an expert in Currency Trading from Madrid that one can use the same Welles-Wilder Indicator to decide when to buy and sell Currencies as well as for opening Options positions. One outstanding advantage of currency trading is the great leverage of one's capital. For example, one may buy or sell one "lot" of currency with a trading account of only $1,000 where the value of one lot is close to $100,000.

This book will show you how to make your capital grow safely using the above strategies. The Credit Spread strategy provides a steady monthly income that increases with your capital growth. The Debit Spread strategy uses a computed market signal called the Welles-Wilder Indicator (a relative strength indicator) to find targets of opportunity to augment your monthly income above the steady income. This Welles-Wilder Indicator is a signal when to open a position for potential profit for a few trading days at a time.

A method of using the Welles-Wilder Indicator to decide when to buy and sell High Technology Growth stocks is described. The possible profits of buying and holding growth stocks for long term is also presented.

The book presents you with all the equations and algorithms used in my Self-Adaptive Trading Software using Microsoft Windows/Excel programs so you may create your own software on your personal computer. A number of sample charts and spreadsheets that you may create with your own software are presented.

In order to avoid filling the book with outdated charts, I have limited the charts to one per chapter. All the up-to-date charts are available from the author by sending an email request for **Self-Adaptive Options & Currency Charts.** This file will be sent to you as an email attachment for a small handling fee. My email address is: jonsch1@verizon.net

CHAPTER 1

INTRODUCTION TO TRADING IN MARKETS OF: INDEX OPTIONS, FUTURE OPTIONS, TECH STOCKS & OPTIONS, & CURRENCIES

The September 11, 2001, disaster caused all the markets to drop with extreme volatility. This sudden turn of events made the options market change drastically as the stock market suffered a major sell off. The new market situation forced me to review the market strategies I was using before 9-11 and adapt to the new conditions. It caused me to learn new ways to build up my investment capital. The final result is I have devised new and better ways to make capital grow rapidly, and I have adapted the old strategies to the new market conditions. I learned that currency trading nicely complements options trading and provides another means of leveraged capital growth. Furthermore, I discovered that one of the powerful market signals described in my previous books works as well for currency trading as for options trading. This market signal is the Welles-Wilder Indicator (WWI) which tells when to open a potentially profitable Debit Spread. This WWI trigger can be applied to widely traded Stock and Commodity Futures Options, and to World Currencies.

I refer to this change in tactics as Self-Adaptive trading. When I was chief engineer for Rockwell International for the F111 fighter aircraft, I had a patented control system for that aircraft called the Self-Adaptive Autopilot, which used high frequency interrogational signals to test the sensitivity of the control surfaces of the aircraft to the changing aerodynamic conditions the aircraft experienced during its wide range of altitudes and airspeeds. This interrogation provided Self-Adaptive changes of the autopilot loop gains, thereby maintaining stability of the aircraft with no other outside sensors necessary to measure temperature, air pressure, etc. In other words, the aircraft would self adapt to the changing conditions it experienced. My USC doctoral thesis detailed this Self-Adaptive autopilot and its principles.

My plan is to explain to you how you may adapt your trading strategies to making money in the volatile markets of the 21st century. As a result of the new options and currencies trading strategies, I have developed a new Windows/ Excel-based software program that makes it easy to apply these strategies in the real world of options and currencies. I have learned by about two years of paper trading these new strategies that Currency trading is the simplest, has only one strategy and requires the least capital, or about $4,000, to begin trading. OEX and Stock Options are more complex than Currencies since there are four strategies that are profitable and require about $5,000 capital to begin trading. Futures Options is the most complex and requires about $5,000 capital to start.

UNDERLYING MARKETS

This book will cover five market areas: Index Options, Stock Options, Commodity Futures Options, four of the major World Currencies, and several Tech Stocks. The WWI is the unifying market signal used to decide when to open options positions or when to buy and sell currencies. In the fifth market area of trading the Tech Stocks, I researched two methods: using WWI signals for buying and selling the stocks, and just buying and holding the stocks for a year. All five areas work well.

I have found that My Yahoo covers all the options and currency data. You can easily customize your My Yahoo website to include the OEX and Stocks that you are interested in trading. There are, of course, many other Internet trading websites which will be covered in Appendix A, but I feel one needs a personalized website like My Yahoo to use daily for market data and to give a daily market overview to the active trader. The book describes two basic strategies: (1) two sigma covered credit spreads for generating monthly income, and (2) debit option spreads for OEX and the future options, long stock options, currency trades and buying and selling stocks triggered by the Welles-Wilder Indicator (WWI).

The book also describes the software I use in my actual and paper trading. The equations used in this software are included in the book so you can build your own software. If you need help with any of the equations, I am available by email. The software available from me is described in the Chapter 12. It allows you to trade four markets using the above two basic strategies: (1) OEX Index Options and more than a dozen Stock Options; (2) Commodity and Futures Options; (3) Currency Trading for Euro/$, Swiss Franc/$, Yen/$, British Pound/$, and a Yen-Euro Hedge; and (4) Buying and Selling 200 Shares of several Tech Stocks—*or you may concentrate on one of the 4 market areas.* The software tracks the underlying markets and computes the 2 sigmas. The WWI spreadsheets use a logic equation to determine when a Put or Call Debit spread is triggered. Another feature you can get from me is an up-to-date list of charts of the OEX Index, 13 stocks, 10 Futures, and 4 Foreign Currencies/$ plotted with the underlying market and the Welles-Wilder Indicator. These charts are not included in the book because they go out of date so quickly. A few examples will be included to show you what the charts look like.

A Quick Overview of the Strategies:

Two Sigma Call Covered Credit Spread: Sell the Call options at the strike price two standard deviations (2 sigma) above the market and buy the same number of Call options the next strike price higher than the Short Call strike price. This position results in an Initial Credit. If the market expires below the Short Call, the Initial Credit received when the position is opened becomes profit. *This position is opened at the beginning of each option month to generate a monthly income.*

Two Sigma Put Covered Credit Spread: Sell the Put options at the strike price two standard deviations (2 sigma) below the market and buy the same number of Put options the next strike price lower than the Short Put strike price. This position results in an Initial Credit. If the market expires above the Short Put, the Initial Credit received when the position is opened becomes profit. This position is opened at the beginning of each option month to generate a monthly income.

Call Debit Spread triggered when WWI < 20: Buy Call Options at-the-money and sell Call options at the next strike price above for a net debit. If the market rises as the WWI predicts it will, then a profit will result when the position is closed, unless option premium decay causes a loss. *This position is a target of opportunity triggered by the WWI.*

Put Debit Spread triggered when WWI > 80: Buy Put Options at-the-money and sell Put options at the next strike price below for a net debit. If the market drops as the WWI predicts it will, then a profit will result when the position is closed, unless option premium decay causes a loss. *This position is a target of opportunity triggered by the WWI.*

Long Call triggered when WWI < 20: Buy Call Options at-the-money for a net debit. If the market rises as the WWI predicts it will, then a profit will result when the position is closed, unless option premium decay causes a loss. This works for the OEX and the Tracked Tech Stocks. *This position is a target of opportunity triggered by the WWI.*

Long Put triggered when WWI > 80: Buy Put Options at-the-money for a net debit. If the market drops as the WWI predicts it will, then a profit will result when the position is closed, unless option premium decay causes a loss. This works for the 13 Tech Stocks. *This position is a target of opportunity triggered by the WWI.*

The Software described in Chapter 12 has a sheet for OEX Index Options and each of the following 13 Tech Stock Options:

1. Amgen
2. Cisco
3. Dell
4. DNA
5. eBay
6. Intel
7. IBM
8. MSFT
9. NFLX
10. Oracle
11. QQQQ
12. SINA
13. Yahoo

I change the individual stocks from time as market opportunities arise.

Index Options

Many daily financial newspapers provide a list of 19 or more options; however, only five of these index options have a wide spread of options strike prices with good trading volume. Of these five, I find that the S&P100 (OEX) is the best for options trading. The OEX is best because it has the most complete range of options strike prices, the highest volume, and highest open interest (the number of open options positions). The other four index options are: S&P500, Dow Jones Industrials, NASD 100, and SemiconIdx. Typical values of these five indices are:

S&P 100 (OEX)	550	
S&P 500 (SPX)	1,100	
DJInds (DJI)	105	(1/100th of DJIA reported value as posted in options tables)
NASD 100	2,000	
SemiconIdx (SCX)	380	

Which of these index options are suitable for Options Trading?

The first three index options usually have most of the volume and open interest. However, the OEX is the best to trade for two reasons: (1) it has strike prices 5 points apart which permits easy opening of the desired position regardless of the trading strategy used; and (2) it has good premiums for the 2 sigma credit spread which yields better monthly income than the other index options.

Stock Options

More than 516 stock options are traded regularly. I have filtered through this large list searching for those stocks which are actively traded and have selected the 13 stocks listed above which have good trading volume and good option premiums for the Long Calls and Puts triggered by WWI.

I recommend watching the stock market news on CNBC TV which has realtime indexes and streaming realtime quotes for NYSE and NASDAQ stocks. The 13 stocks listed above appear frequently in the streaming quotes. These 13 active stocks are included in my software for computing the WWI market signal, the "trigger" that tells when to open and close a stock option position. Also, a chart for each underlying market is included with the market value and the Welles-Wilder Indicator. A special spreadsheet is provided which computes when the WWI triggers a Long Call or Put options position. I recommend the use of Interquote website, http://cgi.interquote.com/cgi-bin/quotes/qs which provides realtime quotes for OEX, the stocks, and options for OEX and the stocks. You may use this feature to do realtime trading during the trading day or for opening a position the next trading day after a trigger is obtained.

NEURAL NETWORK INDICATOR

I have devised a neural network indicator using 5 weighted inputs of 3 layers with an output that predicts *up trends, down trends or trendless* movements of the market. The 5 inputs are the following market indicators: MAD4, MAD9-4, MADC, Stochastics %K-%D, and WWI for the OEX index. These market indicators as well as the Neural Network are described in detail in Chapter 9. I believe this neural network indicator gives a unique edge to OEX option traders who are trying to fathom the market trends during the 21st Century.

FUTURES OPTIONS

The Orion Futures website (www.orionfutures.com) provides a complete list of futures in the areas of Currencies, Energies, Financials, Grains, Indices, Meats, Metals, and Softs for a total of 80 futures. By clicking on *options* in the futures market values, one may display the available options for a given future and/or commodity options. I sorted through this impressive list to select the futures options with the best selection of options strike prices, the highest trading volume, and the largest open interest for options trading. These *best 10 futures options* are:

1. Kansas City Wheat
2. Corn
3. Soybeans
4. Coffee
5. Gold
6. Crude Oil
7. SPX futures
8. US Treasury Bonds
9. 10-Year Treasury Notes
10. Japanese Yen Futures

These best futures options are described in Chapter 6 and are included in my software for signaling when it would be profitable to open a position such as a WWI-triggered Debit Spread. SPX futures is the best futures options for using the 2 sigma covered credit spread position for generating a monthly profit and it works very similarly to the OEX 2 sigma Credit spreads described in Chapter 5.

CURRENCIES FOR TRADING

My Yahoo website includes four major world currencies which are suitable for trading. All are the currency per the US dollar (the amount of the currency that can be purchased with one US dollar). A Currency expert from Madrid with whom I taught a short course on trading recommended the following list:

1. Euro/$
2. Swiss Franc/$
3. Japanese Yen/$
4. British Lb/$
5. Yen-Euro/$ Hedges

It may surprise you that the Swiss Franc (CHF) is one of the currencies traded since Switzerland is such a small country. This is because of the huge financial influence Switzerland has on the world markets because, historically, the world's most wealthy people have kept their funds in Swiss banks. The Union Bank of Switzerland (UBS), headquartered in Zurich, Switzerland, is one of the most powerful banks in the world, now with branches in the US. The amount these currencies are traded 24 hours per day is enormous. The My Yahoo website presents the NY closing prices daily, even though the currencies continue trading on the London, Frankfurt, Singapore, Hong Kong and Tokyo markets around the clock.

I have discovered that the WWI market signal can be used to trigger when to buy or sell a currency. Currencies are traded in "lots." The approximate value of a Lot in the underlying currency is listed here. Euro: lot size 100,000, value about $100,000; Swiss Franc: lot size 125,000, value about $90,000; Yen: lot size 15,000,000, value about $125,000; British Pound: lot size 75,000, approximate value is $120,000. The margin amount required in a currency trading account to buy or sell one lot of currency is $1,000. Typically a currency position is open for three days, making a profit of $1,000. So you may see this represents a large leverage factor.

However, I recommend you have at least $4,000 in your currency account to trade one lot. This higher amount in your account would reduce the possibility of a Margin Call if the market moved in the wrong direction for a few days. The ratio of value of 1 Euro Lot to equity in account = $100,000/$4,000 = 25.

The use of currency hedges in trading will be discussed in Chapter 7 in which two different currencies are used. I have found the best hedge is buying one lot of Euros and selling one lot of Yen simultaneously, which is known as a Yen-Euro Hedge. Chapter 7 provides a complete description of using WWI as a trigger for buying and selling currency lots for the four currencies and the yen-euro hedge.

How Does the WWI Trigger Work?

The WWI trigger works as follows: (1) when the WWI > 80 this is the trigger for opening a Put Debit Spread or Long Put Stock Option or for selling a Lot of Currency. (2) when the WWI < 20 this is the trigger for opening a Call Debit Spread or Long Call Stock Option or for buying a Lot of Currency. It is a simple signal that results in a profit about 70% or 80% of the time. Losses occur when WWI signals a position but then remains above 80 or below 20 for many trading days until the options premiums decay. I use the **triad** to limit the loss in this case. The position is closed after three days of the WWI remaining in the extreme up or down levels. The WWI Trigger works best when the WWI switches from 80 to less than 60 or switches from 20 to 40 or more in a few trading days.

OPTIONS VOCABULARY

There are a few basic terms used in options trading that should be understood by the options trader. These terms will be defined below - with some practical examples to illustrate their use.

Puts and Calls

Puts and Calls are the fundamental terms for options trading:

A **Put option** increases in value when the underlying market drops or decreases when the market rises. A **Call option** increases in value when the underlying market rises or decreases when the market falls.

Strike Price

Puts and Calls have **strike prices** which is a term that specifies the distance the Call or Put is from the market. OEX options strike prices have values which are normally 5 points apart, such as 100, 105, 110, 115, etc. In some cases, stock options have strike prices that are 2.5 points apart, such as 20, 22.5, 25, 27.5, 30, for eBay. Some options are only one point apart, such as 29, 30, 31, 32, for QQQQ. Some of the futures options, such as wheat, have strike prices 10 points apart, such as 290, 300, 310, 320. The US Treasury Bonds and Notes have strike prices 1 point apart.

Also a complicating factor of futures options is that they have different values per option point. For example, the grain futures options have $50/point. Coffee futures options have $375/point. Gold futures options have $100/point. Crude Oil futures have $1,000/point. SPX futures options have $250/point. US Bond and 10-Year Note futures options have $100,000/point. Yen futures options have $1,250/point.

A further complicating factor for futures options is that some options have strike prices which are multiples of the underlying futures market prices. For example, coffee futures options have strike prices that are 10 times greater than the underlying futures price, oil futures options strike prices are 100 times the underlying futures, and Yen futures options strike prices are 1,000 times the underlying futures. All of these factors are described in Chapter 6 and are included in my Self-Adaptive Futures Options Software.

Expiration Date

Options have a month from one expiration to the next. The expiration date for options is the third Friday of each month, so sometimes the options month is four weeks long and other times five weeks long. Expiration occurs at 10 minutes after 1600 (4 p.m.) New York time. Index and Stock Options have monthly expiration dates. Commodity Futures Options often have monthly, bi-monthly or quarterly expirations depending on the future. That is why options expiration in some months is called *triple witching* when both stock and futures options expire on the same third Friday of the quarterly months. One nice feature of the Orion Futures website futures options quotes is the number of days until expiration is included for each option month .

Expiration Value

At expiration, all Call options with a strike price *greater* than the underlying market become worthless. All Call options with a strike price *less* than the underlying market become = market level minus the Call strike price. For example, if the Call strike price is 485 and the underlying market at expiration = 502.49, then the Call 485 = 502.49 - 485 = 17.49 at expiration. If the Call strike price is 505, then Call 505 = 0 or worthless at expiration.

At expiration, all Put options with a strike price *less* than the underlying market become worthless. All Put options with a strike price *greater* than the underlying market become = Put strike price minus market level. For example, if the Put strike price is 510 and the market at expiration = 502.49, then the Put 510 = 510 - 502.49 = 7.21 at expiration. If the Put strike price is 495, then Put 495 = 0 at expiration.

These expiration values for Puts and Calls can be used to generate profits when using some of the strategies explained in this book. For example, the Call and Put credit spreads yield a profit of the initial credit when the underlying market finishes between the Short Call and Short Put. This profit occurs because the strike prices become worthless at expiration.

You should note the strike prices of Puts and Calls have opposite characteristics with respect to market movements and to the market value at expiration.

Option Value Relative to the Market

The value of Call strike prices decreases as the strike price is *greater* than the underlying market value. The value of the option strike price is referred to as the premium when the Call strike price is greater than the market value. Typically the premium value decreases exponentially as the distance *above* the market increases, becoming zero at large distances *above* the market.

The value of Call strike prices increases as the strike price is *less* than the market. The Call strike price has two components: the premium value and the inherent value. The *inherent value* is the difference between the market value and the Call strike price = market minus Call strike price; the premium value is the difference between the Call strike price value and the inherent value. For example, if the market value is 502.79 and the Call at strike price 490 has a value of 13.25, then the inherent value = 502.79 - 490 = 12.79 and the premium value is 13.25 - 12.79 = 0.46.

The value of the Put strike prices decreases as the strike price is *less* than the underlying market value. The premium value of the put strike price decreases exponentially as the distance *below* the market increases, becoming zero at large distances *below* the market. The Put strike price value below the market is the premium value.

The value of the Put strike price increases as the strike price is *greater* than the market. The Put strike price value also has inherent and premium values. The *inherent value* is the difference between the Put strike price and the market value = Put strike price minus market value; the premium value is the difference between the Put strike price value and the inherent value. For example, if the market value = 502.79 and the Put strike price 505 is 3.10, then the Put 505 inherent value = 505 - 502.79 = 2.21 and the Put 505 premium = 3.10 - 2.21 = 0.89. Again, you may observe the Puts and Calls have opposite characteristics.

The basic approach in options trading is to profit from the dynamics of Call strike price values and Put strike price values. We shall examine strategies to take advantage of both the short-term and long-term movements of the markets.

Now that you understand what the *premium* value is for Put and Call options, you can observe that the *premium* values *increase* when the volatility of the underlying market *increases* and conversely decreases with less market volatility. The options selected for presentation in this book tend to have high volatility. High volatility benefits the options trader because it increases the premiums and yields larger profits for the risks you take. A measurement of market volatility is given by the *index VIX* which is typically about 16.

Short Positions

The options trading strategies in this book involve buying and selling Calls and Puts. The term *Short* means a Put or Call that is *sold.* When you sell a Put or Call you *receive the value* of the option strike price. So a Short Call means a Call you sold. A Short Put means a Put you sold. In the strategies discussed in this book, you will use Short Calls and Puts for two purposes:

1. To generate a credit for an option position for credit spreads.
2. To reduce the cost of an option position opened for debit spreads.

Long Positions

The term *long* means a Put or Call that is *bought*. When you buy a Put or Call, you *pay* the value of the option. So a Long Call means a Call you bought. A Long Put is a Put you bought. In the strategies discussed in this book, you will use Long Calls and Long Puts for two purposes:

1. To protect a Short Call or Put in order to limit the loss for an unfavorable market move for credit spreads.
2. To buy a Put or Call at a lower cost than the amount you will sell the Call or Put for in the future in order to generate a profit when you sell it.

At-the-Money (ATM) Positions

This term is used to denote Calls or Puts having a strike price closest to the underlying market. For example, if the underlying market is 502.79, the ATM Put would be a Put with a strike price at 505. The ATM Call would also have a strike price of 505. A strike price of 500 would be 2.79 from the market whereas the strike price of 505 is only 2.21 from the market. In this book, we will examine strategies which use ATM Calls and Puts, namely the WWI triggered Call or Put Debit Spreads or Long Calls or Long Puts. In the case of the 13 Tech Stocks, ATM Long Calls or Long Puts will be used when WWI triggered.

Out-of-the-Money (OTM)

This term is used to denote Calls or Puts having strike prices which have *no* inherent value. In other words, an OTM Put would be a Put with a strike price *less* than the market; an OTM Call would be a Call with a strike price *greater* than the market. If the underlying market is 502.79, then OTM Calls would be Calls with strike prices 505, 510, 515, etc. The OTM Puts would be Puts with strike prices 500, 495, 490, etc. We will look at strategies in this book which use OTM Calls and Puts, principally the 2 sigma Call and Put Covered Credit Spreads for generating a monthly income.

In-the-Money (ITM)

This term is used to denote Calls or Puts having strike prices which have both inherent and premium value components. For example, if the underlying market is 502.79, then ITM Calls would be Calls with strike prices 500, 495, 490, etc. ITM Puts would be Puts with strike prices 505, 510, 515, etc. We will examine strategies in this book in which we open ATM Calls or Puts and expect the market to move so that the ATM Calls or Puts become ITM Calls or Puts to generate a profit.

Margins for Options Trading

Margins are the amount of funds required in your trading account to permit you to trade options positions having a short position that would lose cash if the market moved in an unfavorable direction. The margin represents cash to protect the broker in case of an option position loss. The equations for computing the margins are given in Chapter 2. In the case of Currencies, the margin is the amount that the broker requires to buy or sell one lot of currency, which is normally $1,000. For five OEX short spread options with OTM strike prices (that is, Short Calls with Long Calls 5 points greater or Short Puts with Long Puts 5 points less), the margin = $2,500 for the Call and $2,500 for the Put. Typically, the Initial Credit would be $350 for a five options of a 2 sigma Call or Put credit spread, so the typical monthly yield would be 14% or an annual yield of 168%. This example demonstrates the leverage of option trading.

Day Trading Requirements

Day trading is defined as opening a position and then closing the same position during the same trading day. I do not recommend day trading. The SEC requires that anyone doing day trading have a minimum of $25,000 in his or her broker's trading account.

OEX OPTION CODES

Market brokers and the websites that provide realtime or near realtime options data normally use letter codes to represent Put and Call numerical strike prices and the expiration month for the option. The codes below are for OEX positions with 5 point differences between strike prices, but other options have similar codes. There is a three letter code to tell which 100 the OEX position is in plus a two letter code to represent the month and the last two digits of the strike price. On the Internet, B & J Brokers, CBS Portfolio and Interquote Portfolio have symbol search provisions for determining the proper symbol code. For example, in the case of the B & J brokers, if you use the "trade" selection of their web page and chose "spread," then you enter the underlying market, then on the spread page, you select the Call or Put strike price from a list of available strike prices for "Buy to Open" and for "Sell to Open" with the number of options, and whether the spread is a "credit" spread or a "debit" spread. Then the next window provides the codes for each side of the spread.

Month Codes for Puts and Calls

Month	JAN	FEB	MAR	APR	MAY	JUN
Call code	A	B	C	D	E	F
Put code	M	N	O	P	Q	R

Month	JUL	AUG	SEP	OCT	NOV	DEC
Call code	G	H	I	J	K	L
Put code	S	T	U	V	W	X

Strike Price Codes (For the last two digits of OEX)

A	B	C	D	E	F
05	10	15	20	25	30
G	H	I	J	K	L
35	40	45	50	55	60
M	N	O	P	Q	R
65	70	75	80	85	90
S	T	U V W X Y Z			
95	100	Not used for strike prices			

Some Example Codes: If the underlying market is 502.79

The code		
	GA = July Call 505	SA = July Put 505
	GB = July Call 510	SB = July Put 510
	GC = July Call 515	ST = July Put 500
	GF = July Call 530	SR = July Put 490
	GG = July Call 535	SP = July Put 480
	JB = Oct Call 510	VH = Oct Put 440
	LD = Dec Call 520	XL = Dec Put 460

As you may see, if the strike prices are more than 100 points apart, there could be an ambiguity. For the OEX, three letters have been chosen to represent each 100 as follows:

For Strike Prices from	300 to 395, use OEW
	400 to 495, use OXB
	500 to 595, use OEB
	600 to 695, use OEY
	700 to 795, use OEZ
	800 to 895, use OEX

For other options there are different letter groups. For example, for the QQQQ there are different letters to go with the different spaces between strike prices:

For Strike Prices from	25 to 34, use QAV
	35 to 60, use QQQ
	61 to 73, use QUE
	74 to 80, use YQQ

In the case of Interquote, which provides realtime option portfolio quotes, the three letter code is written first, followed by a space and then the two-letter code. For example, the January Call 510 would be written OEB AB and the April Put 390 would be written OEW PR. In the case of B & J Options Brokers Internet ordering page, there is no space between the letters so the two examples above would be written OEBAB and OEWPR. In the case of the CBS Portfolio, which is a 20-minute delayed free Portfolio service, the code for the two OEX examples above would be written as OEB=AB for Jan Call 510 and OEW=PR for April Put 390.

Here is a test for the meaning of the OEX codes. The answers are in Appendix C1.

1. What is OEY CD?
2. What is OEB WE?
3. What is OEW QQ?
4. What is OEB OS?
5. What is OEY AP?

Currency Vocabulary

I will be discussing four foreign currencies: Euro, Yen, Swiss Franc and British Pound Sterling. I chose these four foreign currencies for the simple reason they are the most active *freely traded* currencies in the world. China, for example, supports their currency at a fixed amount, so it is not freely traded. If in the future China should release their currency to the free markets of the world, then it would certainly become among the currencies to trade.

The exchange rate for the currencies chosen is how many of the foreign currency that can be purchased for one US dollar. For example, an Euro exchange rate of 0.8212 means for one dollar you can buy 0.8212 euros. A Yen exchange rate of 112.36 means for one US dollar you can buy 112.36 Japanese Yen. In currency trading you either buy or sell one Lot of the foreign currency.

Lot size is the principal term in currency trading. When buying or selling currencies you specify the currency and the number of Lots you are buying or selling. It is necessary to have a currency broker and a trading account open. You must have a minimum of $1,000 in your account for each Lot you buy or sell. As I stated previously in this chapter, I recommend a minimum of $4,000 in your currency trading account. There are some excellent Internet currency brokers, such as www.forex.com, where you can place your orders to buy or sell a specified number of Lots of whatever currency. Such orders can be made by using the www.forex.com currency trading web page for entering the trading parameters such as: the currency; whether to buy or sell; the number of Lots; your account number code and the price you expect to receive if it is a sell order or the amount you are willing to pay if it is a buy order. If you specify a "market" buy or sell, that indicates you are willing to accept the market price rather than your own specified price for the currency. The currency Lot value is the value in the foreign currency. The value for Lots of my four chosen foreign currencies are given below:

1 Lot of Euros = 100,000 European Union Euros

1 Lot of Swiss Francs = 125,000 Swiss Francs

1 Lot of Yen = 15,000,000 Japanese Yen

1 Lot of Pounds = 75,000 British Pounds

Currency brokers don't charge commission, instead they make their money by the 3 to 5 blips between buying and selling. Blips are 0.0001 of a Euros, Swiss Franc, British Pounds, or 0.01 of a Yen.

Some Example Currency Computations Are:

Buy 3 Lots of Euros at 0.8750 or less. If filled, your account would be debited by the amount = 3 * $100,000/0.8750 = $114,286*3 = $342,857 and you would be required to have a minimum cash in your account = 3 * 1,000 = $3,000. This represents a leverage of 114 to one.

Sell 2 Lots of Yen at 119 or more. If filled, your account would be credited with the amount = 2 * 15,000,000/119 = $2 * 126,050 = $252,100. You would need a minimum of $2,000 cash in your account to make this transaction—a leverage ratio of 126 to one.

Buy 4 Lots of British pounds at the market price. A few seconds after placing your internet order you would receive confirmation that your order was filled at the market price of Pound = 0.6292, and your account was debited by the amount = 4 * 75,000/0.6292 = 4 * 119,199 = $476,796. To make this trade you would have had to have a minimum of $4,000 cash in your trading account—a leverage ratio of 119 to one.

Buy one Lot of Euros at 0.8800 and after executed sell 1 Lot of Euros at 0.8700. A half hour later you would receive confirmation that your buy order was filled at 0.8800 as specified. An amount = 100,000/0.8800 = $113.636 would be debited from your account. To place this buy and then sell order, you would have needed a minimum of $2000 cash in your account: $1000 for the buy and $1000 for the sell. Two hours after receiving the buy confirmation you could receive notice that your sell order was filled at a price of 0.8700. Your account would be credited with a value = 100,000/0.870 $ 114,942. Your profit for this buy and then sell transaction = $1,306 for a minimum cash amount of $2,000. So the return = 1306/2000 = 65.3%, a good return for two hours. In the actual examples given in Chapter 7, the typical Currency trade lasts 3 days.

Sell 3 Lots of Yen at an exchange rate of 118.5 and after executed Buy 3 Lots of Yen for 119.0. Five minutes after placing the sell order on your broker's website, you would receive confirmation that you sold 3 lots of Yen at 118.5 and your account was credited with the amount = 3 * 15,000,000/118.5 = $379,747. An hour and a half later you could receive notice that your buy order for 3 lots of Yen at 119.0 had been filled. Your account was now debited by the amount = 3 * 15,000,000/119 = $378,151. Your profit for this round trip sell/buy = $379,747 - 378,151 = $1,596. You would need to have a minimum of $3,000 cash for the Sell order and $3,000 cash for the Buy order or a total minimum cash of $6,000. Your return on cash = 1,596/6,000 = 26.6%.

I believe the last two trading examples illustrate that, for small amounts of cash in your currency trading account, you may make high percentage returns on your capital with round trip buy/sell or sell/buy transactions. This book will show you a way to decide when to make potentially profitable buy/sell orders using the WWI market signal. Your work is to enter daily the New York closing prices into currency trading spreadsheets for the four major currencies: the Euro, Swiss Franc, Yen and Pound Sterling. Also, we will examine techniques of using two of these currencies in a buy/sell transaction called Currency Hedges to make good profits using the WWI signal to decide when to open the Hedge position.

Here is a test for computing values of Currency Lots. Answers in Appendix C2.

1. How much does it cost to buy 3 lots of Euros at 0.8123 Euro/$?
2. How much cash is required in your account to buy 3 lots of Euros?
3. How much cash is required in your account to sell 2 lots of British Pounds?
4. How much credit is received when you sell 5 lots of Yen at 117.90 Yen/$?
5. How much cash is required in your account to sell 2 lots of Swiss Francs?

Objective of Options and Currency Trading

My basic objective of options trading is to use the OEX 2 sigma Covered Credit Spreads to generate a monthly profit and augment this monthly income by taking advantage of *targets of opportunity* uncovered by the WWI telling when to open OEX & Future Call or Put Debit Spreads or ATM Long Stock Options. The Future Options can also use both the 2 sigma Covered Credit Spread and the WWI triggered Debit Spreads. The Covered Credit Spread strategy for Future Options is complicated by the fact there are bi-monthly or quarterly expiration dates. However, SPX Future Options have monthly expirations with 5 points apart strike prices and may be used similarly to the OEX Index Options. Also, you may use WWI as the trigger for when to buy and sell the four major currencies to generate profits.

Capital Growth Models

Capital growth models are discussed in Chapters 4 through 8 and are included in the author's software packages. The capital growth model should be used in two ways: (1) to provide an ideal, if unachievable, goal for your trading, and (2) to keep track of your actual trading results as you progress along the path of options and currency trading. It is always more difficult to do actual trading when you are using your real money than the paper trading used as the basis for many of the examples in this book.

Conservative Capital Growth with Low Risk: OEX & Stock Options

The conservative capital growth model uses a fixed number of options based upon the initial amount of capital in your options and currency trading accounts. The number of options remains the same for one year at a time. The projected capital growth is computed for 12 months. Beginning with $20,000 capital using 10 OEX Credit Spreads for a profit $1,000/mo, at the end of a year of trading the $20,000 has grown to $32,000 for an annual return of 60%. The margin required for these 10 credit spreads remains at $10,000 which is 50% or less of the trading capital. This mathematical model of capital growth is simplistic in that it assumes the same amount of return or profit each month and the same number of options each month. At the end of one year the number of options is increased to 16 options with a monthly profit of $1,600. At the end of the second year the trading capital has grown from $32,000 to $51,000. So the initial capital of $20,000 has grown to $51,000 for an average annual growth rate of 127.5%

Aggressive Capital Growth with Moderate Risk

The aggressive capital growth model starts with 10 options based on the initial $20,000 trading capital but increases the number of options by two quarterly as the amount in the trading account grows from quarter to quarter. Because the number of options is adjusted quarterly, the aggressive capital growth model grows faster than the conservative model in which the level of trading is only adjusted annually.

During the first quarter the monthly profit is $1,000, the second-quarter monthly profit is $1,200, the third-quarter monthly profit is $1,400 and the fourth quarter monthly profit is $1,600. At the end of the first year the capital has grown from $20,000 to $36,600 for an annual growth of 78%.

During the second year, the first-quarter monthly profit is $1,800, the second-quarter the monthly profit is $2,000, the third-quarter monthly profit is $2,200 and the fourth-quarter monthly profit is $2,400. This model shows a second-year profit of $25,200, making the trading capital $61,800 at the end of two years. So the initial capital of $20,000 has grown to $61,8000 for an average annual growth rate of 104.5%.

Aggressive Capital Growth with One Loss per Quarter

To give more reality to the capital growth model we assume that once per quarter there is a loss of a fixed number of points or varying dollar amounts depending on the number of options traded. The losses are expressed in points of the option profit. For example, it is assumed that for a normal month the OEX covered credit spread has a profit of 1.0 points The loss for the OEX is assumed to equal -0.5 points. Also the model assumes the stock option profit is one half the OEX point profit. So if the normal profit for the OEX is 1 point, then the quarterly loss would be -.5 points. For the first year of the aggressive capital growth model starting with $20,000 trading capital, the first-quarter profit = $1,500; the second-quarter profit = $1,800; the third-quarter profit = $2,100; the fourth-quarter profit = $2,400 for a first-year profit = $7,800, making the trading capital at the end of the year = $27,800 for an annual growth rate = 39%.

During the second year of the aggressive capital growth model, the first-quarter profit = $2,700; the second-quarter profit = $3,000; the third-quarter profit = $3,300; the fourth-quarter profit = $3,600 ,for a second-year profit = $12,600 making the trading capital = $40,400 for an annual growth rate = 45%. For the two years the trading capital grew from $20,000 to $40,400 for an average annual growth rate of 50%. A quarterly loss is more often than I have actually experienced.

When the market moves up or down more than 2 sigma during the option month, then the Short Call or Put will be threatened and corrective action must be taken to reduce the potential loss. This type of threat happens a few times per year. The corrective action consists of closing out the threatened credit spread and then opening a new, safer credit spread with the Short Call higher, or the Short Put lower. The loss can be further reduced by closing the unthreatened credit spread and opening a new position closer to the market on the unthreatened side of the market. This corrective action, which normally results in a net loss for the option month, will be necessary two or three times per year.

SUMMARY

This book covers four different market areas for making profits by leveraging your trading capital. In all the strategies described in the book, I strongly urge you to use only 50% of your trading account capital for margin:

1. OEX Index Options and Stock Options
2. Commodity and Future Options
3. Currency Trading of four Foreign Currencies per US$
4. Buying and Selling 200 Shares of Tech Stocks

I have filtered through numerous index options, stock options, and future options to select the best options for trading because of high volume and wide range of strike prices.

I will share with you new strategies in trading Index Options and Stock Options that I learned through research in actual and paper trading over the several years since I returned to California to add to what I learned during the 15 years living in Spain and trading Options in London. Each chapter will discuss different aspects of market trading and will show you how to build your own Excel trading software.

This first chapter is the introduction to the Options and Currency Markets.

Trading Strategies for Options and Currencies will be discussed in Chapter 2.

Chapter 3 shows how to compute the key trading parameters.

Chapter 4 discusses various ways to trade OEX options.

Chapter 5 discusses strategies to profit from 13 growth stock options.

My paper trading of Futures options has taught me the ropes of this complex market segment. I have learned which are the best to trade and what hazards to avoid which I will share with you in Chapter 6.

I was assisted by an expert currency trader from Madrid who has had years of currency trading experience to pick the four best currencies to trade. He was delighted to learn that my strategy of using the WWI to trigger Buy and Sell signals worked for currencies as it works for options. I've been paper trading currencies for over two years and expect to begin real trading using an internet broker such as www.mgforex.com or www.saxobank.com soon. I will share with you what I've learned about currency trading in Chapter 7.

Chapter 8 covers how to profit from Buying and Selling 200 Shares of the 10 Tech Stocks, which is an easy way to invest a few thousand dollars and get profits as good as the top growth Mutual Funds such as CGM Focus.

Chapter 9 will cover some other market signal indicators I have used in the past. I find with my new strategies that I can trade without these more complex market indicators. Five of these signal indicators have been combined through the power of *a 5 input, 3 layer neural network* to indicate market trends for the OEX: uptrend when the neural network (NN) signal is >10, downtrend when the NN signal is <-10, and a trendless market when the NN signal is between 10 and minus 10.

In Chapter 10 I will give you some trading tips I have learned over the last 18 years of trading that may help you increase your profits and decrease your risks.

Chapter 11 will present the computations for a Global Capital Growth model for four years of trading and for individual models for each of the 4 market trading areas covered by this book.

In Chapter 12 I will explain how my new Self-Adaptive software can be used to aid you in generating profits on your trading capital using the strategies described in this book. This software is simplified from the Oexstrgy I previously offered when I lived in Spain. I think the stock and future markets have a reviving dynamism. Many people are going to renew the wealth they lost after the severe drop in the market since 9-11 using strategies described in this book.

I plan to make my trading capital grow through options and currency trading using the mathematically sound strategies presented in this book. I'm proud to apply the mathematics I learned at the California Institute of Technology (Caltech) where I earned my BS in Physics in 1951 and at the University of Southern California (USC) where I earned my Ph.D. in EE and Mathematics in 1963. In past years I was proud to use my academic knowledge designing Avionics and Missile Systems to protect our country against overseas threats to our people's security. Now I expect to use my mathematical knowledge to make my future life more comfortable through Options and Currency trading. I hope you can use these strategies to make your trading capital grow at a faster rate than more conventional investments.

CHAPTER 2

OVERALL STRATEGIES FOR TRADING INDEX, STOCK & FUTURE OPTIONS, CURRENCIES & STOCKS

There are two basic types of options strategies that will be presented in this chapter:

1. **Covered Credit Spreads** that use Short Calls two standard deviations (2 sigma) above the market with a cover of the same number of Long Calls one strike price higher; and Short Puts 2 sigma below the market with a cover of the same number of Long Puts the next strike price lower. These credit spreads use options which expire during the current options month. Index Options and Stock Options, and SPX Future options expire on the third Friday of the month. The Covered Credit Spreads are used to generate a regular monthly income.
2. **Debit Spreads** or **Long Calls** or **Puts** are used to augment the monthly profit when the WWI signals that a debit spread may be profitable. Debit Spreads use Long Calls or Puts At-the-Money (ATM) and Short Calls or Puts one strike price above the Call Debit spreads or one strike price below the Long Put Debit spreads. In some cases, ATM Long Calls and Long Puts are used for stock options or futures options when the cost/profit ratio is beneficial. The Long Calls or Puts make more profit for a given movement in the underlying market value. Debit spreads are used because the opening cost is considerably less than for the Long Call or Put because the Short Call or Put reduces the number of points for a position.

When Do You Open These Positions?

The 2 sigma Covered Credit Spreads are opened near the beginning of the new options month because the short Premiums and therefore the Initial Credit is greater at that time. The Initial Credit decreases as the number of days until expiration decreases.

The Debit Spreads (or Long Positions) are opened only when the WWI triggers the position with a high probability of earning a short-term profit. A Call Debit Spread or a Long Stock Call is opened when WWI < 20; A Put Debit Spread or a Long Stock Put is opened when WWI > 80.

When Do You Close These Positions?

The Short Calls are selected at two standard deviations (2 sigma) above the market and the Short Puts are selected at 2 sigma below the market, so that the credit spreads become worthless at expiration if the market behaves normally. Therefore, the Initial Credit received when the credit spread is opened becomes the Profit when the options expire at close on the third Friday of the options month, unless there is an unusually great rise or drop. In the case of an unusual rise which threatens your Short Call, you must take corrective action, close the Call Covered Credit Spread and open a new higher Call Spread. In the case of an unusually large drop which threatens your Short Put, you must take corrective action by closing the Put Covered Credit Spread and open a new lower Put Spread. Therefore you don't need to close the credit spread if the market remains between the Short Call and the Short Put strike prices as it does during normal market variations. Normally the Call and Put Covered Credit Spreads will expire worthless, leaving your initial credit as profit for the Option Month.

The Debit Spreads (or long positions) are normally closed after a few days to realize a good profit based on the initial cost when the position was opened. You should have a profit objective when the position is opened. When the market moves such that the profit objective is met, the position should be closed. This is accomplished by giving an order to the broker to close the position at your profit objective after the Debit Spread is opened. This close order is placed using a good-til-canceled (GTC) order. The hazard for Put Debit Spreads is that the WWI of the underlying market occasionally remains *hung-up* above 80 for several days in which case the Debit Spread may suffer a loss. I use the **triad tactic** of closing the Put Debit Spread (or Long Put) if WWI > 80 after three days to limit the loss.

A similar hazard for Call Debit Spread is if the WWI remains *stuck-down* below 20 for several days a loss may occur. This hazard is combated with the **triad tactic** of closing the Call Debit Spread (or Long Call) if WWI < 20 after three days to limit the loss.

THE NAKED SPREAD STRATEGY

The Chicago Board of Options Exchange (CBOE) has a requirement that your account must have a minimum balance of $50,000 for you to open an OEX naked spread position. So if you are starting out options trading with a more modest amount, you will have to use the other strategies described in this book until your capital grows to $50,000.

I was introduced to options trading using this naked credit spread strategy in 1986 on a beach in Brest, France. I was watching my oldest son racing 40-foot catamaran sailboats off the coast of France. Bob, the sponsor of my son's sailboat, was an options trader from New York, and I had been told that he was earning over a million dollars in profit per month doing options trading. I asked Bob if he would explain his system to me. For the next hour in the warm sun on the Brest beach, he explained his naked spread strategy while I took notes.

He used Index Options because they had large trading volumes and high open interest. He explained that for the large number of options he was trading, it was important to use index options with high volume so his orders would not influence the market and his entry orders would be quickly and easily filled. The naked spread strategy was opened normally on the first day of the new options month with index options that expired at the end of the new options month which would be the third Friday of the next month. His explanation is below:

How to Open a Naked Credit Spread

First you must compute the two sigma, usually written 2sig, which is two times the Standard Deviation of the index option for the up variation for the Call 2sig and for the down variation for the Put 2sig. The standard deviation computations are based on the maximum up variations for the last 13 options months and the maximum down variations for the last 13 options months. In my "100% Book," I used 13 months for the 2sig, but the extreme volatility after the September 11 disaster caused me to reduce to seven months. Now, however, the volatility has reduced, so 13 months is again usable. The volatility caused by the disaster made the 2sig so large and far from the market that the strike price premiums were so small there was no way to make money at those far-out positions.

The standard deviation is a statistical function given by Microsoft's Excel spreadsheet program. That is the formula I use to compute the Call 2sig and the Put 2sig.

Make your order to your broker. Remember, SHORT is when you SELL an option:

Sell a number of Call options with Call strike prices equal to the market PLUS the Call 2sig

AND at the same time Sell the same number of Put options with Put strike prices equal to the market MINUS the Put 2sig.

How Much Credit Do You Receive When You Open the Naked Credit Spread?

The Initial Credit equals the number of options ordered times the dollars per point times the sum of the Call strike price premium plus the Put strike price premium.

How Much Profit Do You Earn at the End of the Options Month?

If the market remains between the Call strike price and the Put strike price, then the monthly profit is the same as the Initial Credit received when the position was opened.

Statistically speaking, by using Short Calls and Puts which are 2sig from the market, the probability of the market remaining less than the Short Call and more than the Short Put is 95%. If you had only $50,000, you could open only four options as in the example below.

After my quick introduction to the naked spread strategy, I called my London broker to obtain option premiums my first naked spread position for 10 Index Options. The initial credit was $11,000 for this paper trade which ended as profit at expiration in the first options month. I was sold on this strategy. When I returned home to Malaga, Spain, I used our personal computer to write a BASIC Language computer program for trading index options. Since my trading was a profit success, I wanted to share my newfound knowledge, so I wrote my first options book, *The Insiders Automatic Options Strategy*, which was published by Windsor Books.

Examples of Naked Credit Spreads Using 4 OEX Aug 2003 Options

For the OEX, the Call 2sig = 31.1 and the Put 2sig = 37.4

On Monday of the July 2003 options month, data from the IBD (International Business Daily) Index Options section, OEX = 492.80, change - 8.70, high = 501.5, low = 491.16. This made the volatility difference = 501.5 - 491.16 = 10.34. I call this difference the **daily swing.**

The OEX Call 2sig strike price = 492.80 + 31.1 = 523.9, Round off to the nearest Call strike price = Call 525

The OEX Put 2 sig strike price = 492.8 - 37.4 = 455.4, Round off to the nearest Put strike price = Put 455.

Using the Closing Prices for Aug C525 = 1.05 and Aug P455 = 1.4. The Initial Credit = #Ops * 100 * (Cprem + Pprem), which means the number of options times the dollars per point times the sum of the Call premium plus the Put premium which equals = 4 * 100 * (1.05 + 1.4) = $980 - commission, using B&J(my present broker)'s internet commission of $8.50 per option. The credit received in your options trading account = $985 - 8.5 * 8 = $912. To make this trade, you must have a minimum of $50,000 in your trading account.

The return on Margin = $912 divided by $50,000 = 1.8%/month = 21.9%/year

The naked spread has a Margin that must be computed. Margin = 25% of the market value times the number of options times the dollars per point. For the OEX example above, the margin = 4 * 100 * 0.25 * 492.8 = $49,280. So, in this example, the margin for the naked spreads was less than the $50,000 minimum.

The Covered Spread Strategy

The covered credit spread strategy is similar to the naked spread strategy with two main differences:

1. The margin required in your trading account is much less than for the naked spread. The margin = N (number of options) * $/point * (short minus long strike price difference). So for 10 options, 100$/point for the OEX and a difference of 5 points between the Short Call and Long Call, then the Call Margin = 10 * 100 * 5 = $5,000. US brokers require the same Margin for the Put and for the Call side of the Credit Spread, so the total Margin would be $10,000. London brokers only require the Put or Call side for Margin, the rationale being one cannot lose on *both sides!*
2. The short 2sig Put and short 2sig Call are protected by the Long Put and Long Call so that the maximum possible loss is the margin in dollars required to open the position on either the Call or Put side.

How to Open the Covered Credit Spread

As for the naked spread, you must compute the 2sigma for the Call (UP) variation and Put (DOWN) variation using the sum of the UP variations and the sum of the DOWN variations for each month over the last 7 options months. This is the same 2sig calculation as for the naked spreads.

For the Call covered spread, sell a number of Call options at a strike price Call 2sig above the market and buy the same number of Call options at one strike price higher than the Short Call position. *Remember, short is when you sell an option.*

For the Put covered spread, sell a number of Put options at a strike price Put 2sig below the market and buy the same number of Put options at one strike price lower than the Short Put position.

How Much Is the margin for a Covered Credit Spread?

(N = number of options)

Call Margin = N * $/point * (Short Call strike price - Long Call strike price) = 10 * 100 * 5 = $5,000, for 10 options and the spread difference of 5 points, and for the CBOE $/point = 100

Put Margin = N * $/point * (Short Put strike price - Long Put strike price) = 10 * 100 * 5 = $5,000, for 10 options and the spread difference of 5 points, and for the CBOE $/point = 100

In Chicago the total Margin = Call Margin + Put Margin = $10,000.
In London the total Margin = Call Margin or Put Margin = $5,000.

How Much Credit Do You Receive When You Open A 2sig Covered Credit Spread?

The Call Initial Credit = N * $/point * (Short Call premium - Long Call premium) – for CBOE options the $/point = 100. So if the number of options N = 10, and the Premium difference = 0.9 points, then the Initial Credit = 10 * 100 * 0.9 - Comm = $900 - 70 = $830. Or a return on Margin = 830/5000 = 16.6% for the month.

The Put Initial Credit = N * $/point * (Short Put premium - Long Put premium). So if the number of options N = 10, and the Premium difference = 0.9 points, then the Initial Credit = 10 * 100 * 0.9 - Comm = $900 - 70 = $830. Or a return on Margin = 830/5000 = 16.6% for the month.

The total Initial Credit for both the Call and Put sides of the spread are $1,660 or a return on Margin of 1660/10,000 = 16.6% for the month or an annual return = 199%. If you use only half of your trading capital for Margin, this makes the return on capital = 100%/year.

How Much Profit Do You Earn at the End of the Options Month?

If the market remains less than the Short Call and more than the Short Put, then the profit at options expirations (third Friday of the options month) = Call Initial Credit + Put Initial Credit = $1,660 in the example above. Statistically speaking, by using Short Calls and Puts which are 2 sigma from the market, the probability of the market remaining less than the Short Call and more than the Short Put is 95%. *This yields a monthly return on Margin = 16.6%/mo. = 199%/year or a 100% return on trading capital – provided you use only 50% of your capital for Margin.*

Example of a 2-Sided Covered Credit Spread, Using 10 OEX Aug 03 Options

For the OEX, the Call 2sig = 31.1, the Put 2sig = 37.4,

On Monday of the July 2003 options month, data from the IBD (International Business Daily) Index Options section, the OEX = 492.80, a change during that day of - 8.70.

Call 2sig strike price = 492.80 + 31.1 = 523.9, Round off to the nearest Call strike price = Call 525

Put 2sig strike price = 492.8 - 37.4 = 455.4, Round off to the nearest Put strike price = Put 455.

Compute Initial Credit using IBD 21 Jul 03 closing prices.
Init Credit = 10 * 100 * (Call525 - C530 + P455 - P450)
= 1,000 * (1.05 - 0.6 + 1.4 - 1.0) = (0.45 Call + 0.4 Put)
= 1,000 * (0.85) = $850 - commission

Using B&J's internet commission of $35 for each side of the spread, the Initial Credit
= 850 - 2 * 35 = $780

Compute the margin required to Open the Two-sided Covered Credit Spread:
Call Margin = 10 * 100 * (5) = $5,000
Put Margin = 10 * 100 * (5) = $5,000

In the US, brokers require a Margin for *both* sides, Total Margin = Call Margin plus Put Margin = $10,000. In London, the brokers require a Margin on only one side, since the maximum loss could be only one side or $5,000.

The return on Margin
In the US: return = $780 divided by $10,000 = 7.8%/month = 93.6%/year
In London: return = $780 divided by $5,000 = 15.6%/month = 187.2%/year

So, as you may see, the covered credit spread earns excellent returns on the margin required to open the position.

The Debit Spread or Long Strategy

The Debit Spread Strategy uses the Welles-Wilder Indicator (WWI) for telling when a Call Debit Spread or when a Put Debit Spread should be opened. *But first, what is a Debit Spread?*

A **Call Debit Spread** is structured opposite to the credit spread discussed above: Buy Nops (number of options) at the strike price nearest the market and Sell Nops at the next strike price above the Long Call. A Call Debit Spread will be profitable if the market rises from its position when the spread is opened. Normally, a Debit Spread is held for only a few days, because if it is held too many days, the premium decay erases the potential profits. You need to set a profit goal when you open your position.

For example, if the cost of opening the Debit Spread is 2.5, a reasonable profit goal would be to close that position when it reaches a value of 3.0, which would be a profit of 0.5 points. The best way to achieve this goal is to place the close order immediately after the position is opened. This forces your broker to close the position when it reaches your profit goal. You should monitor your position daily to assure the market is moving in the proper direction for a profit. If the value does not increase within three days, then you should consider closing the position at a small loss. The maximum possible loss is the cost of the position.

A **Put Debit Spread**: Buy Nops at the strike prices nearest the market and Sell Nops at the next strike price below the Long Put. A Put Debit Spread will be profitable if the market drops.

How Do We Use the WWI to Tell When to Open a Debit Spread or Long Option Position?

When WWI < 20: Open a Call Debit Spread, because the WWI is telling us that the market is oversold and will rise.

When WWI > 80: Open a Put Debit Spread, because the WWI is telling us that the market is overbought and will drop.

As mentioned above, the hazard is when the WWI is *hung-up* above 80 for more than three days for a Put Debit Spread or *stuck-down* below 20 for more than three days for the Call Debit Spread. The **triad tactic** is used to limit the loss in these two conditions by closing the Debit Spread after three days.

Long Stock Calls: For the 13 common stocks covered in this book, the WWI < 20 is a signal that buying a Stock Call at-the-money may be profitable if the market rises as the WWI predicts it will.

Long Stock Puts: For the 13 common stocks covered in this book, the WWI > 80 is a signal that buying a Stock Put at-the-money may be profitable if the market drops as the WWI predicts it will.

The cost of Long Calls or Puts for stocks is much less than the cost of Long Calls or Puts for index options or for futures options. Therefore it is feasible not to have a Short Call above the Long Call or a Short Put below the Long Put to reduce the cost of the position, as in the Debit Spreads described above

Currency Trading

The four major world currencies covered in this book also use the WWI for deciding when to Buy or Sell the Currency. When WWI > 80, Sell the Currency. When WWI < 20, Buy the currency. When a profit is made, close the long or short Currency position. In other words, if WWI signals you to Buy, after a few days and a profit has been earned, then sell the currency to close the position. Also if WWI signals you to Sell, after a few days and a profit has been earned, then buy back the currency to close the position. *Currency brokers don't charge commission; instead they make their money by the 3 to 5 blips between buying and selling. Blips are 0.0001 of a Euro, Swiss Franc, British Pound, or 0.01 of a Yen.*

Stock Trading

Chapter 5 discusses trading Options for the 13 Tech Stocks.

Chapter 8 covers the same 13 Tech Stocks but uses two other strategies to profit from these stocks:

Use WWI to decide when to Buy and Sell 200 shares of the stock for short-term profits.

Buy and Hold the Stocks for a year to profit. My research shows that these 13 stocks earned more profit by buying and holding than most Mutual Funds for the year Oct 02 to Oct 03.

SUMMARY

This chapter surveys the strategies used for trading Index Options, Stock Options, and Future Options, Currencies and Stock Trading.

The OEX Index Options and 13 Tech Stock Options are used to generate trading profits using 2 sigma covered credit spreads for Index Options, Stock Options, and SPX Future Options for a monthly income and using WWI-triggered Stock Options for the 13 Tech Stocks whenever the stocks are overbought or oversold.

The four Currencies can be traded by Buying one Lot of the Currency when WWI < 20 and Selling one Lot of the Currency when WWI > 80. These are short-term trades for a few days with a required Margin of only $1,000.

Chapters 4 through 8 of this book cover in detail the strategies of trading surveyed in this chapter.

CHAPTER 3

HOW TO COMPUTE KEY TRADING PARAMETERS

To be a successful options and currency trader, it is necessary to keep a daily log of those underlying markets and currencies you are trading. This requires entering the NY closing prices of the index, stocks, futures and currencies you are trading. Even though the currencies are traded 24 hours per day, the 4 PM NY closing prices are used. This task of data entry normally takes about a half hour. You should have an automated spreadsheet program such as Excel to make all the computations using your entered data. The computations that should be computed include the market signal indicators you use for your trading decisions.

This chapter provides you with the concepts, algorithms and equations required to create the automated spreadsheets needed. Microsoft Excel spreadsheet program, which operates under Windows, contains all the features required to implement the spreadsheets and charts. A separate spreadsheet should be created for each Index, Stock, and Future for whose Options you plan to trade. Also, a spreadsheet should be made for each Currency and Currency Hedge you want to trade. These spreadsheets are the basis for Time Charts. Excel has easy-to-use chart generation features to aid you in visualizing the market and market signal variations. The charts can be made in multicolor for viewing on your desktop or laptop personal computer. For those of you so inclined, the equations and algorithms presented in this chapter will permit you to create your own Excel workbooks. It is easy but time consuming.

As an alternative, I have created four separate software packets which are described in Chapter 12. This package of programs is called *Self-Adaptive Stock and Future Options and Currency Trading* and is available as four email attachments including the User's Manuals. You may order this software from my email: jonsch1@verizon.net for a modest price. Also, a monthly update is available for a small annual cost which includes the latest data updates, charts adjusted for the next Option Month, plus any enhancements that may be given to the software during the year. The monthly update is delivered to subscribers on the weekend after the third Friday Options Expiration. This service assures you have all the data needed to open new market positions for the next Option Month.

Exponential Moving Average Algorithms

One of the most useful algorithms is the set of equations used to compute the exponential moving average. No matter how many days the moving average is for, the equations only require two days of information: today's and yesterday's. This makes it very convenient to compute the exponential moving average using a spreadsheet program such as Excel. The exponential moving average uses two factors: factor f1 and factor f2, where f1 + f2 = 1. The equations for f1 and f2 are given below:

f1 = 2/(n + 1), where n = number of days for the moving average

f2 = 1 – f1 = 1 – 2/(n + 1)

The Welles-Wilder Indicator (WWI) uses the 7-day exponential moving average, or n = 7. For this case:

f1 = 2/(7 + 1) = 2/8 = ¼ = 0.25
f2 = 1 - f1 = 1 - ¼ = ¾ = 0.75

How Do We Compute the 7-Day Exponential Moving Average of the up and down Change Used in the WWI?

Multiply today's OEX change in the closing value times f1 and add that to f2 multiplied by yesterday's exponential moving average value. If OEX changed up by 1.25 today and yesterday's 7-day moving average was 7.25, then what is today's 7-day moving average?

Today's 7-day exponential moving average = 0.25 * 1.25 + 0.75 * 7.25 = 5.75

How Do We Compute the 50-Day Exponential Moving Average for the OEX to Use as a Trigger?

Multiply today's OEX closing value times f1 and add that to f2 multiplied by yesterday's exponential moving average value. (This same formula can be used for 25-day, or any other number, exponential moving averages by changing the number for n.)

n = 50, so f1 = 2/51 = .03922, f2 = 1 - f1 = 1 - .03922 = 0.9608

In this next example, assume today's OEX = 500, and yesterday's 50-day OEX exponential moving average = 493.20.

Then today's OEX-day ExMovAvg = 500 * .03922 + 493.2 * .9608 = 519.97

As you may see, it is easy to compute any moving average using the exponential moving average algorithm. Excel makes it very simple.

Welles-Wilder Indicator (WWI)

The WWI was described in my previous options book, *100% Return Options Trading Strategy*, as a Relative Strength Indicator. When the WWI based on the 7-Day Exponential Moving Average is greater than 80, this is a signal that the market is overbought and will fall back soon. When the WWI <20, this is a signal that the market is oversold and will rise soon. In my previous options book, I didn't appreciate the powerful tool this indicator was in making market decisions. As we have seen in Chapter 2, the WWI is a very strong trigger in deciding when to open a Debit Spread, Long Call or Put, or buying and selling currency lots.

EQUATION FOR 2 SIGMA

The summation of the Up movement of the market for the Option Month, and the summation of the Down movement of the market for the Option Month are computed for each Option Month. Here are two typical computations using the Excel SUM function. C247:C267 means the up movement values for OEX during a typical Option Month, which is either 4 or 5 weeks, which were shown in cells 247 through 267 in Column C in my OEX spreadsheet. Cells 247 through 267 in Column D in the same spreadsheet show the down movement values for OEX for the same Option Month. Use the following Excel function to sum these numbers:

Up summation: = SUM(C247:C267) = 40 for a typical OEX Option Month
Down summation: = SUM(D247:D267) = - 45 for a typical OEX Option Month

To compute the Call 2sig and Put 2sig, use the Up summation and Down summation for the last several months. The following example from the period after the 9-11 disaster uses 7 for the number of months, as you need to do whenever the volatility is extremely high. The equations are shown below:

Call 2sig: = 2 * STDEV(M6:M12) = 16.34, where STDEV is the Excel standard deviation (sigma) function and M6:M12 are the 7 cells in Column M where the Up summations are stored.

Put 2sig: = 2 * STDEV(N6:N12) = 15.68, where N is the Down summation Column.

As a result of these standard deviation values, the 2sig Short Call was computed to be: OEX 2sig Short Call = 5 * ROUND((B268 + M20)/5,0) = 540, so the Long Call = 545, the next strike price higher. B268 is the cell containing the OEX value, M20 is the cell containing the C 2sigma value.

OEX 2sig Short Put = 5 * ROUND((B268 - N20)/5,0) = 505, the Long Put = 500, the next strike price lower. B268 is the cell containing the OEX value, N20 is the cell containing the P 2sig.

WWI Computations for OEX

Computation of Up movement: = IF((B268 - B267) > 0,B268 - B267,0) = 3.31, where B268 has today's OEX, B267 has yesterday's OEX. IF is the Excel If function.

Computation of Down movement: = IF((B268 - B267) < 0,B268 - B267,0), where B268 has today's OEX, B267 has yesterday's OEX. IF is the Excel If function.

UP 7-Day Exponential Moving Average = E267 * 0.75 + C268 * 0.25, where E267 is yesterday's 7-Day MovAvg, C268 is today's UP and .75 is the 7-day f2, and .25 is the 7-day f1.

DOWN 7-Day Exponential Moving Average = F267 * 0.75 + D268 * 0.25, where F267 is yesterday's 7-Day MovAvg, D268 is today's DOWN and .75 is the 7-day f2, and .25 is the 7-day f1.

WWI = 100 * (E268/(E268 - F268)), where E268 is today's UP 7-day MovAvg and F268 is today's DOWN 7-day MovAvg.

The equations in the section above are used for an OEX 2sig covered credit spread and the WWI computation is used for Debit Spread triggers.

OTHER MARKET SIGNAL INDICATORS

Note, you may obtain a free set of the charts listed in this section my emailing me at jonschl@verizon.net and asking for third book market indicator charts as an attachment.

Although the WWI is the most powerful signal indicator for telling you when to open Debit Spreads or Long Positions, there are a number of other market indicators that aid the active options trader in maintaining a global view of market behavior. They can also be applied to stocks, commodity futures, and currencies. I have decided not to use these other signal indicators and their charts in my trading software because, for me, too much information can be distracting. Nevertheless, I do maintain a spreadsheet computing these indicators. A quick review of these signal indicators and their equations will be presented below. In each case, when a moving average is used in the indicator, *the exponential moving average* will be used. For each example presented below, the OEX is used as the underlying market; however, any of the Stocks, Futures or Currencies could be used as well. *Also, I generate a time chart for each signal indicator versus OEX. This spreadsheet named SelfAdaptSigIndicOEX is provided free to people who order my trading software.*

FOUR-DAY MOVING AVERAGE DIFFERENCE=MAD4

The equation for the 4-day moving average is = SF4 * B265 + (1 - SF4) * I264, where B265 contains today's OEX, SF4 is the 4-day moving average factor1 = 2/(4 + 1) = 0.4 and 1 - SF4 is factor2 = 1 - 0.4 = 0.6; I264 contains yesterday's 4-day moving average.

The equation for the MAD4 = B265 - I265 where B265 contains today's OEX value and I265 contains today's computed 4-day exponential moving average.

Difference Between the 9-day and 4-day Moving Averages = MAD9-4

Another signal indicator is the difference between the 9- and 4-day exponential moving averages or MAD9-4. The chart for this signal indicator is given in Chapter 9. The equations for this indicator are given below.

The 4-day exponential moving average is the same as above. The 9-day exponential moving average equation is: = D269 * $F$3 + F268 * $F$2, where cell F3 contains f1 = 0.2 the 9-day factor 1 and cell F2 contains f2 the 9-day factor 2 = 0.8. The equation for the MAD9-4 is given by: = D269 - F269, where D269 contains the 4-day moving average and F269 contains the 9-day moving average.

The Moving Average Difference Comparison = MADC

This market signal indicator compares the 20-day and 10-day exponential moving averages, takes the 13-day exponential moving average of the difference between the 20- and 10-day moving averages, and then takes the difference between OEX and the 13-day moving average difference. The equations are below:

The 20-day exponential moving average equation is: = $H$3 * B269 + H268 * $H$2, where H3 and H2 contain f1 and f2 for 20 days: f1 = 2/(20 + 1) = 0.0952 and f2 = 1 - f1 = 0.905; B269 contains the value of OEX, and H268 is yesterday's 20-day moving average for OEX.

The 10-day exponential moving average equation is: = B269 * $I$3 + I268 * $I$2, where I3 and I2 contain f1 and f2 for 10 days: f1 = 2/(40 + 1) = 0.1818 and f2 = 1 - f1 = 0.8181: B269 contains the value of OEX, and I268 is yesterday's 20-day moving average for OEX.

The equation for the MAD20-10 moving average difference is: = I269 - H269, where I269 is the 20-day moving average and H269 is the 40-day moving average.

The equation for the 13-day exponential moving average of the Mav20-10 is: = J269 * $K$3 + $K$2 * K268, where J269 contains today's difference, and K268 is yesterday's 13-day moving average of the difference. Cells K3 and K2 contain f1 and f2 of the 13-day exponential moving average: f1 = 0.1428 and f2 = 1 - f1 = 0.8571

Finally, the equation for the Market Indicator MADC is given by the equation: = J269 - K269, where J contains the MAD20-10 and K is the 13-day moving average of MAD20-10. I used this market signal indicator for many years for trading the OEX.

THE STOCHASTICS %K - %D MARKET SIGNAL INDICATOR

The Stochastics %K - %D signal indicator is the most complex of the signal indicators. This indicator requires 9 Columns on the Excel spreadsheet to compute its value. This segment of the spreadsheet is discussed below:

M N O P Q R S T U

The first two Columns, M and N, compute the 5-day Max and Min for the OEX (or underlying market). The next two Columns, O and P, compute the 3-day exponential moving average of the difference between OEX and 5-day Min and the difference between the 5-day Max and Min. The next Column, Q, computes the 3-day exponential moving average of the ratio between Columns O and P. The next Column, R, computes %K, which is the difference between the OEX (or underlying market) and the 5-day Min. The next Column, S, computes %D, which is the ratio between Columns O and P. The next Column, T, computes the 3-day exponential moving average of %K in Column R. The Stochastics %K - %D is computed in the final Column, U, which is the difference between Columns R and T.

Complex Market Signal Indicators

I am always amazed at how I learned all of these complex market signal indicators while I was living in Spain. One of the readers of my first options book, *The Insider's Automatic Options Strategy*, an elderly Chinese gentleman named Samn, from San Francisco, began communicating with me by email. He liked my book, but believed I needed to use more complex market signal indicators. So we began a transatlantic technical conversation by email in which he gave me the algorithms for the Stochastics %K - %D, MADC, and many others which I incorporated into my Oexstrgy and SamnMod software packages that I formerly offered while I lived in Spain.

As with many of the complex algorithms incorporated in that older software, I have concluded after over a year of intensive research that the Welles-Wilder Indicator (WWI) is suitable for making trading decisions for the OEX, the 13 Tech Stock Options, the 9 Future Options, and the 4 World Currencies covered in this book. I have presented you the algorithms of some of these other market signal indicators in this chapter . More of these market signal indicators are presented in Chapter 9. Also, as a bonus to anyone who may order any of my Self-Adaptive Trading software packages, *I will include free the software package called SelfAdapSigIndicOEX* (which includes these complex signal indicators) if you order any of my Trading software packages. This Excel workbook also includes a page with a 6 input, 3 layer Neural Network for signaling an Up or Down trend or a trendless market of the OEX. The OEX is an excellent trendsetter for the overall market.

SUMMARY

This chapter reviews the algorithms used in the computations for the strategies in this book. I have also showed how to lay them out on Excel spreadsheets, how to use the various functions supplied as part of the Excel program, and how to fit the numbers into the formulas and Excel functions.

* I gave you the 2 standard deviation calculations used for the 2sig Short Calls and Short Puts to be used in the Covered Credit Spreads
* Included were the formulas needed for the Long Calls and Puts used as covers in the Covered Credit Spreads
* I explained the algorithms for the Welles-Wilder Indicator (WWI) used as a Trigger in the Debit Spreads, Long Stock and Stock Option Positions, and the Currency Lot Buying and Selling for profitable trading.
* I have also shared the algorithms for some of the complex market indicators to give you an understanding of these other indicators that I no longer use for making trading decisions. These were the equations I learned from Mr. Samn of San Francisco almost 20 years ago.
* I discussed in Chapter 1 and will also include in Chapter 9 what I learned from my recent academic research on Neural Networks applied to OEX Options.

CHAPTER 4

OEX INDEX OPTIONS

The OEX Index Options are the *bread-and-butter* options to use to generate a steady monthly income using the 2 sigma Covered Credit Spread Strategy (CCSS) explained in Chapter 1. This strategy should make a *monthly profit 10 months per year* and *2 months of loss for a net annual profit.* Losses can occur when the market moves drastically and threatens the Short Call or Short Put. When such a threat occurs, you should consider closing the threatened side and open a new CCSS a safe distance from the market. This *protective action* will be explained fully in Chapter 10. *You must adjust yourself psychologically for occasional losses.*

The OEX Index Option can also be used to generate supplementary profits using the Debit Spread Strategy (DSS) when the Welles-Wilder Indicator (WWI) shows that the market is oversold (WWI < 20) or overbought (WWI > 80). *Oversold implies an imminent market rise; overbought implies an imminent market drop.* This short-term strategy in which the DSS is open for a few trading days can add to the CCSS monthly income.

Another OEX options strategy is the 2 sigma Naked Short Credit Spread (NSCS) which is a riskier strategy than the CCSS or the DSS strategies because the loss can be unlimited if there is a sudden drop caused by a disaster such as the 9-11 terrorist attack or the market collapses of October 1987 or October 1929. The CBOE requires a minimum of $50,000 in your trading account before this naked spread strategy can be used. Briefly, this strategy involves selling OEX Calls at Strike Prices 2 sigma above the market and selling an equal number of Puts at Strike Prices 2 sigma below the market.

Examples will be given of trades using each of the three strategies in this chapter. Finally we will present a trading model for OEX CCSS and OEX DSS strategies as your goal for your own trading assuming you begin with $25,000 Capital in your options trading account.

USE OF THE 2 SIGMA (2 STANDARD DEVIATIONS) FOR SPREADS

I use two standard deviations, also called 2 sigma, to choose where to place my covered spreads. Standard deviation is a statistical measure that makes the covered spread positions safe 95% of the time (assuming the market is a purely random process).

The OEX 2 sigma computations are based on the maximum and minimum levels reached during the Option Month (third Friday to third Friday). The maximum of the Up movements and the minimum of the Down movements are maintained daily on an Excel spreadsheet used for computing the WWI for trading. To compute the 2 sigma, use the following steps:

1. Use the following Excel equation to obtain the Option Month Maximum:
   =SUM(C97:C117)
   where Column C in the Excel spreadsheet contains the daily Up movements and rows 97 through 117 are cells containing the daily Up movements for a complete Option Month.

2. Use the following Excel equation to obtain the Option Month Minimum:
   =SUM(D97:D117)
   where Column D in the Excel spreadsheet contains the daily Down movements and rows 97 through 117 are cells containing the daily Down movements for a complete Option Month.
3. Tabulate these computed Maxima and Minima for a series of consecutive Option Months.
4. Use the Excel standard deviation equation for a series of consecutive Option Months to compute:

* the Call Standard Deviation: 2 Sigma = 2 * STDEV(M9:M21), where cells M9 through M21 contain the monthly maxima
* the Put Standard Deviation: 2 Sigma = 2 * STDEV(N9:N21), where cells N9 through N21 contain the monthly minima

Rows 9 through 21 contain 13 consecutive Option Months, including the latest Option Month.

5. A good trader will also compute 2 sigmas for 9 months, 6 months, and 3 months so that shorter periods can be used during times of extreme volatility to compensate for the large increases in the 13-month 2 sigma caused by such unusual market volatility. The equations for the Call 2 sigmas for the monthly periods of 9, 6, and 3 months are given below for the same ending month:
   * 13-month 2 Sigma = 2 * STDEV(M9:M21)
   * 9-month 2 Sigma = 2 * STDEV(M13:M21)
   * 6-month 2 Sigma = 2 * STDEV(M16:M21)
   * 3-month 2 Sigma = 2 * STDEV(M19:M21)

The 6-month 2 Sigma is a good compromise to use during periods of high volatility.

You should create a spreadsheet with all of the OEX computations shown above. These parameters are tracked in my SelfAdaptiveStkOp software. Typical 6-month values are:

* Call 2 sigma = 20
* Put 2 sigma = 25

The Put 2 sigmas tend to be larger because drops are larger and more rapid than rises.

The spreadsheet segment computations for the 2 sigma Call and Put Covered Credit Spread are shown below. Using the value of OEX at the third Friday expiration of the options month, the following computations are made to establish the two-sided Covered Credit Spread positions for the coming options month:

* OEX = 515, number options = 10, number $'s per point = 100
* Short Call = 515 + C2sig = 515 + 20 = C535, Premium = 1.9
* Long Call = 535 + 5 = C540, Premium = 1.2
* Call Covered Spread Initial Credit = 10 * 100 * (1.9 - 1.2) = $700; Margin = 5 * 100 * 10 = $5,000
* Short Put = 515 - P2sig = 515 - 25= P490, Premium = 2.1
* Long Put = 490 - 5 = P485, Premium = 1.4

* Put Covered Spread Initial Credit = 10 * 100 * (2.1 - 1.4) = $700; Margin = 5 * 100 * 10 = $5,000
* % Return on Margin = 100 * ($700 + $700)/($5,000 + $5,000) = 14%

The New Month position is opened by Selling 10 C535 and 10 P590 and Buying 10 C540 and P585 which will have a total Initial Credit = $1,400, requiring a total Margin of $10,000.

Also, the 2-sided OEX Naked Credit Spread is computed on the same spreadsheet to yield the following:

* OEX = 515, number options = 10, number $'s per point = 100
* Short Call = 515 + C2sig = 515 + 20 = C535, Premium = 1.9
* Call Naked Spread Initial Credit = 10 * 100 * 1.9 = $1,900
* Short Put = 515 - P2sig = 515 - 25= P490, Premium = 2.1
* Put Naked Spread Initial Credit = 10 * 100 * 2.1= $2,100
* Minimum Margin = $50,000; %Return on Margin = 100 * $2,100/ $50,000 = 8%

The New Month position is opened by Selling 10 C535 and 10 P590 for a total Initial Credit = $4,000, requiring a total Margin of $50,000

Based on the percent return on Margin, the OEX 2 sigma Covered Spread is more cost effective than the 2 sigma Naked Spread.

You may configure your *my.yahoo.com* website to give you free options premium values, delayed 20 minutes, with accurate closing values, as soon as 20 minutes have passed after market close. For reasons explained in Chapter 1, OEX is the best Index Option to use for the strategies described in this chapter.

The CBOE website: http://www.cboe.com/ is an excellent source of free 20-minute-delayed option chains that can be used in your options trading. To use this site, select Delayed Quotes under the Quotes tab. Then enter in the white box: OEX, and click on List All Options & LEAPS. Next click on the Submit button below to obtain all the Calls and Puts for OEX for the current option month. Then this data can be copied into an Excel spreadsheet. My SelfAdapStkOp software has such a sheet.

How to Compute Standard Deviation & Two Sigma for Covered Spreads

A quick review of the 2 sigma covered credit spread strategies:

Two Sigma Call Covered Credit Spread: Sell the Call options at the strike price 2 sigma above the market and buy the same number of Call options the next strike price higher than the Short Call strike price. This position results in an Initial Credit. If the market expires below the Short Call, the Initial Credit received when the position is opened becomes profit.

Two Sigma Put Covered Credit Spread: Sell the Put options at the strike price 2 sigma below the market and buy the same number of Put options the next strike price lower than the Short Put strike price. This position results in an Initial Credit. If the market expires above the Short Put, the Initial Credit received when the position is opened becomes profit.

So how do we compute the 2 sigma for the Put and Call used in this strategy? This computation is accomplished using a Microsoft Excel spreadsheet and the functions included in Excel and is shown below. This OEX spreadsheet is included in my Self-Adaptive software entitled SelfAdapStkOp. The cells referred to below are the cells in that software.

The 2 Standard Deviation (2 sig) Computations and 2 sig Covered Credit Spread Computations are given in a special segment of the spreadsheet used for tracking the OEX daily.

The Standard Deviation (sig) is computed using Excel's STDEV function using the last 13 months. The two spreadsheet segments go from Column L through N.

The 2 sig Short Call and Short Put strike prices are computed using the following equations:

Short Call = 5 * ROUND((B440 + M24)/5,0), where B440 contains the OEX value at Option expiration and M24 contains the value of the Call 2 sigma computed with the equation: = 2 * STDEV(M9:M21), where M9 to M21 contains the maximum variation of OEX for the option 13 months.

Long Call = M29 + 5, where M29 contains the strike price of the Short Call and it is 5 points to the next higher Call strike price. **Note:** for options that have strike prices closer spaced than 5 points, the 5 would be adjusted accordingly, for example 2.5 for eBay stock options.

Short Put = 5 * ROUND((B440 - N24)/5,0), where B440 contains the OEX value at Option expiration and N24 contains the value of the Put 2 sigma computed with the equation: = 2 * STDEV(N9:N21), where N9 to N21 contains the minimum variation of OEX for the 13 Option Months.

Long Put = N29 - 5, where N29 contains the strike price of the Short Put and it is 5 points to the next lower Put strike price. **Note:** for options that have strike prices less than 5 points apart, the 5 would be adjusted accordingly, for example 2.5 for Intel stock options.

Note: the same information and equations are included in the spreadsheets for the 13 stocks: Amgen, Cisco, Dell, DNA, eBay, IBM, Intel, Msft Nflx, QQQQ, Oracle, Sina, and Yahoo. These stocks are included in the software: entitled SelfAdapStkOp.

Comparison of OEX, SPX & DJIA 2sigma Covered Credit Spreads

I find the 2 sigma Covered Credit Spread Strategy is an excellent method for generating a steady monthly income. I prefer OEX because it has a wider range of strike prices 5 points apart and better volume than the other indexes. However the method works with any index, as shown by the three examples below, all for the same day, to compare trading Covered Credit Spreads using the OEX, SPX, and DJIA Indexes.

These examples use data from the IBD newspaper Options Tables (data in the Tue., 22 Jul 03 issue) for Mon., 21 Jul 03. This date was the first-day of the Aug. 03 options month.

Two sigma OEX Covered Spreads:

OEX = 492.80, Call 2 sig = 30.28, Put 2 sig = 40.62, using 10 covered spreads.

Short Call = 492.8 + 30.28 = 523.08, rounded off to the nearest strike price = Call 525, Premium = 1.05

Long Call = 525 + 5 = Call 530, the next highest strike price which is the *cover* for the short C525, Premium = .60. The Call Covered Credit Spread of C525/530 has an *Initial Credit = 10 * 100 * (1.05 - .6) = $450 - $50 commission = $400.*

Short Put = 492.80 - 40.62 = 452.18, rounded off to the nearest strike price = Put = 450, Premium = 1.0

Long Put = 450 - 5 = 455, the closest lower Put strike price, which has a premium = 0.80. The Put Covered Credit Spread *Initial Credit = 10 * 100 * (1.00 - 0.80) = $200 - $50 commission = $150.*

The Two-sided 2 sig OEX Covered Credit Spread has a total Initial Credit = $550. How much Margin do you need in your account to execute this OEX trade?

The margin = # options * 100$/point * spread width = 10 * 100 * 5 = $5,000 for each side of the trade or the total Margin = 2 * $5,000 = $10,000. *I recommend you have at least double the margin amount in your account to execute this trade or a total = 2 * 10,000 = $20,000.*

Your percent return on Margin for this trade = 100 * 550/10,000 = *5.50%/mo, annualized = 66%/yr.*

Two Sigma SPX Covered Spreads:

SPX = 978.80, Call 2 sig = 60.56, Put 2 sig = 81.24, using the number of covered spreads to keep the 2-sided Margin at $10,000, which will be only *5 options* for reasons shown below:

Short Call = 978.80 + 60.56 = 1039.36, rounded off to the nearest strike price = Call 1050, Premium = 1.10; Long Call next highest strike price = 1075, (there are no strike prices 5 points higher as for the OEX), Premium = 0.40 for a premium difference = 0.70. This wider spread means that in order to limit the Call Margin to $5,000 as for the OEX, then we may open only 2 options rather than 10 options as for OEX. **Note:** Margin = # options * Spread width * $/pt = N * 100 * 25 = 5000, or N= 5000/2500 = 2 options.

The Call Covered Credit Spread *Initial Credit = 2 * 100 * (1.10 - 0.4) = 200 * 0.7= $140 - $Com = $90,* (assume Commission of $50) .

Short Put = 978.80 - 81.24 = 897.56 rounded off to the nearest strike price of Put = 900, Premium = 2.5, the next lower strike price available for the Long Put is at a strike price of Put = 875, with a premium = 1.2, giving a premium difference = 1.30. Since we had to use a 25-point-wide spread in order to keep the margin at $5,000, we can open only 2 Put spreads .

Therefore, the Put Covered Credit Spread *Initial Credit = 2 * 100 * (2.5 - 1.2) = 200 * 1.3= $260 - commission = $210* (assuming $50 commission).

The Two-sided 2 sig SPX Covered Credit Spread has a total Initial Credit = $90 + $210 = $300. Note: this is 83% less the $550 initial credit received for the 10 OEX covered spreads. How much Margin do you need in your account to execute this SPX trade? Margin = $10,000 for both sides of this spread. *I recommend you have at least double the margin amount in your account to execute this trade or a total = 2 * 10,000 = $20,000.*

Your percent return on Margin for this trade = 100 * 300/10,000 = *3.00%/mo, annualized = 36%/yr, considerably lower return than for the OEX.*

Two Sigma DJIA Covered Spreads:

DJIA = 90.97, Call 2 sig = 5.45, Put 2 sig = 7.31, using the number of covered spreads to keep the 2-sided Margin at $10,000, which will be *25 options* for reasons shown below:

Short Call = 90.97 + 5.45 = 96.42, the nearest Call strike price is C96 with a premium = 0.2. The next higher DJ Call strike price = 98, with a premium = 0.1. This narrower premium spread means that if we want to limit the DJ Call Margin to $5,000 as for the OEX, Margin = # options * spread width * $/pt = N * 100 * 2 = 5,000, or N= 5,000/200 = 25 options.

The Call Covered Credit Spread *Initial Credit = 25 * 100 * (.2 - .1) = 2500 * 0.10= $250 - Comm.* The lowest broker commission is $1.5 /option. So for the 2 * 25 = 50 options for the *Call Credit Spread, the commission = $75, so the net Initial Credit after commission = $175.*

Short Put = 90.97 - 7.31 = 83.66, rounded off to the nearest available strike price, Put = 84, Premium = 0.1; the next lower Put strike price is P82 with a premium = 0.15, but the strike prices are 2 points apart meaning we may open only 25 options to keep the margin for the Put side at $5,000. The Put initial credit = 25 * 100 * (0.1 - 0.15) = - $125 – commission. Assuming $75 for commission, then the Put *Initial Credit = minus $200. Therefore the Put side of the DJ Credit Spread would not be opened and the Call Initial Credit = $175 total.*

How much Margin do you need in your account to execute this DJ trade? Margin = $5,000 for the Call side of this spread. *I recommend you have at least double the margin amount in your account to execute this trade or a total = 2 * 5,000 = $10,000.*

Your percent return on Margin for this trade = 100 * 720/10,000 = *7.2%/mo, annualized = 86%/yr.*

As you may see, the OEX was the best trading vehicle for Index Options for this example. My experience has been that OEX has been best for more than a decade for the following reasons:

1. The OEX almost always has strike prices 5 points apart for the 2 sigma strike price range.
2. The OEX has good volume for the options at the 2 sigma strike prices.

Debit Spreads Triggered by WWI for OEX

To compute the WWI using Excel, you should create an 11-Column worksheet with the following Columns:

A	B	C	D	E	F
Date	OEX	Up	Dn	7day Up MA	7day Dn MA

G	H	I	J	K
WWI	Cds < 20	Pds > 80	Cost	Prft

The daily closing data would be entered in the spreadsheet for the OEX (Column B) and Columns C through G would be computed using the equations found in Chapter 3 in the section called "WWI Computations for OEX" (for Columns C through G).

The formulas for each Column are as follows:

The formulas for Columns H and I came from line 455 in the spreadsheet instead of line 268 as used in Columns C through G (just above) to be more up-to-date.

H =IF($G455 < 20,5 * ROUND($B455/5,0),""). A value only shows in the cell in Column H if a Call Debit Spread is indicated because the WWI value in Column G is less than 20.

I =IF($G455 > 80,5 * ROUND($B455/5,0),""). A value only shows in the cell in Column I if a Put Debit Spread is indicated because the WWI value in Column G is more than 80.

The formulas for Columns J and K must be entered by the user because those Columns are only used when one opens or closes a Debit Spread.

J = 1.4 * 10 * 100 + 37, where 1.4 is the premium difference for the Debit Spread, 10 is the number of spreads (Nops) purchased, 100 is the dollars per point, and 37 is the commission paid when the position was opened. The user must enter the correct numbers for the Debit position he or she opens.

K = J435 - J434 - 74, which is the profit when one closes a Debit Spread because the numbers in Column G (WWI) changed from above 80 or from below 20 to the region between 80 and 20 which shows there is no longer an indication the Debit Spread will become more profitable.

So what are the necessary computations for opening and closing Debit Spreads?

Debit Spreads provide a strategy for increasing your monthly income by opening a Call Debit Spread when WWI < 20 or a Put Debit Spread when the WWI > 80. One example of this Debit Spread strategy is given below:

On Monday, 26 September 03, the second Monday of the October 03 Option Month, the OEX closed down 3.67 = 499.61 causing the WWI to reach 19.67, just below the Call Debit Spread trigger level of 20. The At-the-Money (ATM) Call strike price = 500. So the Call Debit Spread = Long Call 500 and Short Call 505. The cost for 10 of these Call Debit Spreads = 10 * 100 * (10 - 7.5) = $2,500 before commission. The 10 is the premium for the C500 and 7.5 is the premium for the C505. The order was placed and filled during the 10 minutes after NY close and before the Chicago Options Close.

The next day, on Tuesday, 27 September 03, the OEX jumped 5.41 closing at 505.02 with the WWI rising to 42.46, a good level to close out the position to take a one-day profit. The order to close was given and executed in the options market 10-minute grace period after NY market close. The value of the 10 Debit Spreads, Long C500, Short C505 = 10 * 100 * (11.37 - 7.3) = $4,070 - $70 round trip commission = $4,000. The net 1-day profit = $1,500 or a return on cost = 1500/2500 = 60.00%.

This Call Debit Spread trading example shows the profit potential for this strategy as an excellent means for augmenting the monthly income of the 2 sigma Covered Credit Spread Strategy. The 2.5 net premium points for opening this position is typical for the OEX. The net profit of 1.5 points is often achievable. However, the growth model in the next section of this chapter assumed only 0.5 profit points per month for the OEX Debit Spreads.

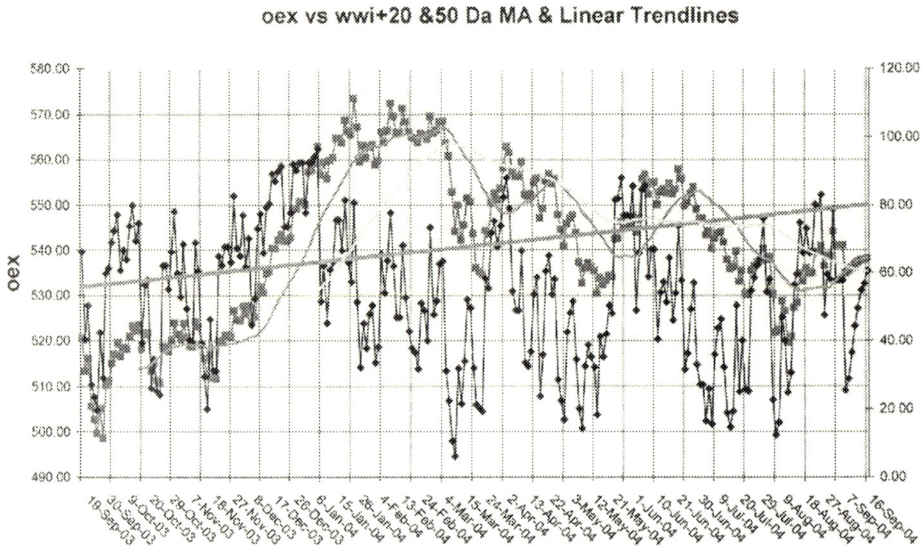
oex vs wwi+20 &50 Da MA & Linear Trendlines
oex
wwi

OEX WWI CHART

The OEX Chart included in the SelfAdapStkOp workbook is shown in the figure above. The curve with the wide swings up and down is the WWI vs Date and the other curve is the OEX. The line is the OEX 20-day Moving Average which is a **trend line** generated by Excel. Also shown are 50-day Moving Average and Linear trend lines.

The big Mutual Fund traders use a similar chart, but they use the 50-day moving average curve instead of the 20-day moving average to decide when to buy and sell stocks; that is to say, when to decide to increase and decrease their overall stock holdings. The OEX spreadsheet can compute the 50-day moving average and OEX and MAD50 curves can be plotted, allowing you to see when the Mutual Fund traders will take action. The MAD50 is the difference between the OEX and the 50-day Moving Average (DMA). When the OEX is above the 50 DMA curve, the market drops, and when the OEX is below the 50 DMA curve, this is a signal for the Fund Managers to increase their holdings, causing the market to rise again. For example, on 30 Sep. 03, the MAD50 was minus 5.03. This was the end of the third quarter when the Fund Managers usually adjust their holdings. This minus 5.03 was a strong signal for them to increase their holdings. As expected, they did, and there was a strong rise in the market on 1 October 03, the first day of the fouth quarter. Some people refer to this market rise on the first day of the new calendar month or new quarter as being foretold by **Chaos Theory**. Now you can predict the Fund Managers actions by using your OEX and MAD50 curves.

OEX Capital Growth Model

Chapter 12 (where the details of the Author's Self-Adaptive Index and Stock Option software package are described) displays the particular Capital Growth Model we have been discussing here. This model assumes you begin with $25,000 Capital in your trading account. Other assumptions include:

1. the 2 sigma OEX CCSS Call ***plus*** Put initial premium points = 0.9 which is a safe estimate.
2. the monthly WWI-triggered DSS total premium profit = 0.5 points.
3. the increase in options increases with 2 each quarter traded and begins with 15 for the CCSS and 10 for the DSS positions.
4. no losses are experienced.

This Model allows the user to compute the parameters for 2 sigma covered spreads for the monthly Covered Credit Spread and the WWI for the Debit Spread triggers for opening a Call or Put Debit Spread. Various results obtained using this capital growth model are shown below:

1. Initial Capital: $25,000
2. First month open 15 OEX two-sided credit spreads, increase number spreads by 2 each quarter, assume 0.9 points for both Call and Put side of the two-sided spreads.
3. First month open 10 OEX Debit Spreads, increase number by 2 spreads each quarter, assume WWI triggers one OEX spread per month with 0.5 points profit for spread.
4. After the first year the Capital has reached $48,857 and the margin has reached $19,000. This is an annual growth rate of95.4%, but requiring only 38.89% of the capital for Margin.
5. After the second year the Capital has reached $78,673 and the margin has reached $23,000. This is an average annual growth rate of 112.97%, but requiring only 29.24% of the capital for Margin. The number of options is 23 for credit spreads and 18 for Debit Spreads.
6. After the third year the Capital has reached $115,433 and the margin has reached $27,000. This is an average annual growth rate of 120.58%, but requiring only 23.39% of the capital for Margin. The number of options is 27 for credit spreads and 22 for Debit Spreads.
7. After the fourth year the Capital has reached $158,689 and the margin has reached $31,000. This is an average annual growth rate of

133.69%, but requiring only 19.54% of the capital for Margin. The number of options is 31 for credit spreads and 26 for Debit Spreads.

8. After the fifth year the Capital has reached $208,441 and the margin has reached $35,000. This is an average annual growth rate of 146.75%, but requiring only 16.79% of the capital for Margin. The number of options is 35 for credit spreads and 30 for Debit Spreads.

This simplistic model shows you can make your capital grow significantly. You must understand, however, that the financial results of this model will only occur if there are no losses.

SUMMARY

OEX Index options provide an opportunity to make your capital grow by over 100% annually using two strategies:

* the 2 sigma Covered Credit Spread
* the ATM Debit Spread Strategy triggered by the WWI.

The Capital Growth Model shows that beginning with $25,000, at the end of the fifth year the capital has grown to $208,441.

CHAPTER 5

STOCK OPTIONS

The 13 stocks listed in Chapter 1 can generate Options trading profits using the same strategies as described for the OEX. All 13 of these stocks are suitable for WWI-triggered Debit Spreads or WWI-triggered At-the-Money Long Positions. ATM Longs are more profitable than Debit Spreads, but cost too much for OEX. The ATM Longs are lower in initial cost for Stock Options than for OEX Index Options because the premiums are lower. The two-sided Covered Credit Spread Strategy (CCSS) or the Naked Spread Strategy can also be used but they are not as safe as the other strategies. These 13 stocks are tracked in my Self-Adaptive Software and are listed in Chapter 1 and repeated here:

1. Amgen
2. Cisco
3. Dell
4. DNA
5. eBay
6. Intel
7. IBM
8. Msft
9. NFLX
10. Oracle
11. QQQQ
12. SINA
13. Yahoo

Three of these stocks (IBM, INTL, Msft) belong to the Dow Jones 30 stocks for the DJIA and the other 10 belong to NASDAQ. All of the stocks are actively traded *high technology* stocks. Amgen is a bio-technology company whose CEO is a graduate of Cal Tech, my alma mater.

I will give examples for WWI-triggered Debit Spreads or Long Calls or Puts for nine of the above stock options. It is feasible to use Long Positions rather than only Debit Spreads because the premiums for ATM Calls or Puts are sufficiently low that the Longs cost less than $2,000. Remember, when WWI > 80 then open a Long Put or Put Debit Spread; when WWI < 20 then open a Long Call or Call Debit Spread. My software has a sheet for each of the 10 stocks.

eBay stock options are the best stock options to use for 2 sigma Covered Credit Spreads. eBay is an actively traded stock and its stock options have good volume and a wide range of strike prices 5 points apart. Most of the stocks have 1, 2.5, or 5 point spreads between strike prices depending on the value of the underlying stock..

IBM is also a possible candidate for CCSS. I believe that using the two-sided Covered Credit Spread Strategy (CCSS) is quite risky for a single stock because favorable or adverse news about the stock can cause wide swings. Nevertheless for those of you may wish to try the 2 sig CCSS for stocks, the 2 sigmas at time of writing for eBay, IBM and QQQQ are given below:

* eBay C2sig = 7, P2sig = 9
* IBM C2sig = 5, P2sig = 7
* QQQQ C2sig = 2, P2sig = 2.5

How Safe are these Stock Covered Credit Spreads?

A snapshot sample of three Covered Credit Spreads for OEX, eBay and QQQQ for the August Option Month: eight days after the spreads were opened, the spreads were safe and all had a positive difference between the Short Call and Short Put. More importantly, the underlying markets for the three (OEX, eBay and QQQQ) finished safe at expiration so the initial credit obtained when the spreads were opened became profit. In this snapshot, the following results were obtained:

1. OEX 10 spreads, C520/525, P490/485, profit = $850, Margin = $10,000, Return on Margin = 8.5%
2. eBay 20 spreads, C117.5/120, P100/97.5, profit = $1320, Margin = $10,000, Return on Margin = 13.2%
3. QQQQ 50 spreads, C33/34, P29/28, profit = $1500, Margin = $10,000, Return on Margin = 15.0%

Stock Splits

If you are ever holding a position when a stock or index splits, the correct adjustments in value will be made automatically. When a stock splits you should go to the beginning of that stock's spreadsheet and split the closing values (Column B) so that there will not be a discontinuity in the charts and WWI computations. If the split is 2 for 1, divide all the previous closing numbers by 2.

To do this, go over to the right on your spreadsheet to an unused Column and label it Split. Put the formula = Bx/2 in the cell in that new Column which is on line x, the line for the day you started keeping data for the stock. Put your cursor on the black plus sign that appears in the lower-right-hand corner when you cover that cell in line x in the new Column and pull down to the date of the split. This will put the formulas in all those cells and make all the new split values appear in your new Column.

Then cover all those new numbers by covering the first number and pulling down with the curser on the middle of the cell. Go to Edit, click on Paste Special, click on Values (because you only want to copy the numbers, not the formulas), move your cursor to Column B, click on the cell on line x, and your new split numbers will replace those previously in Column B. I performed this split operation on my eBay spreadsheet after eBay split in August 03.

At the Beginning of a New Option Month (First Monday after Third Friday Expiration)

At the beginning of the NEW Option Month, you should consider opening a 2 sigma eBay Covered Credit Spread, which has been the best stock for CCSS. Your objective is to open a Call credit spread and a Put credit spread obtaining the greatest initial credit possible. It is *not* necessary to open both the Call and Put sides of the credit spread at the same time or even on the same day.

Here is a tip to increase your monthly profit: check the 2 sig eBay Call and Put Short Strike Prices and Long Strike Prices; check from your market data website the new month's premiums for the four strike prices; insert these values into the Call and Put equations that calculate the Initial Credit that would be received. Rather than use these premiums for the order you place with your website broker, *increase* the value by 0.1 or 0.2 more than is quoted. This way the daily volatility and the increased volatility at the beginning of a new Option Month will help you obtain more initial credit and therefore more profit at the expiration of the new Option Month. The eBay covered spread computations are given below:

Short Call = 2.5 * ROUND((B247 + L20)/2.5,0) - 2.5, where B247 contains the eBay closing prices, and L20 is the Call 2 sigma of 8.02. ROUND is the Excel round off Function.

Short Put = 2.5 * ROUND((B247 - M20)/2.5,0) - 2.5, where B247 contains the eBay closing prices, and M20 is the eBay Put 2 sigma of 4.32.

Call Initial Credit = $L$25 * 100 * (0.35 - 0.1) and the Put Initial Credit = $L$25 * 100 * (0.7 - 0.35), where $L$25 is the cell containing the number of options, 100 is the dollars per point of option, and the numbers in parenthesizes are the net Call and Put short and long premiums.

Total Initial Credit = $460 the net after commission.

Margin is $5,000 = L25 * 100 * 2 * 2.5, where L25 is the number of options = 10, 100 is the dollars per point of option, 2 is for the Put and Call side and 2.5 is the width in points between the short and long strike prices.
The percent return of Initial Credit to Margin = 9.20%.

TARGETS OF OPPORTUNITY: WWI > 80 OR WWI < 20

You should scan your 13 stock spreadsheets daily seeking the WWI triggers which are indicated in Column H for WWI < 20 or Column I for WWI > 80 triggering a potential profitable Call or Put Debit Spread or Long Call or Put. If you decide to open such a position, the Long Call or Put would be At-the-Money, or the strike prices closest to the market.

As shown in the Amgen section below, the spreadsheets for all the stocks have identical formats so the triggers are shown in Columns H and I just to the right of Column G which computes the WWI. The equation for computing the cost of opening 10 Long Calls or Puts is the same as for the Amgen example below but is repeated here: = 10 * 1.05 * 100, where 10 is the number of options, and 1.05 is the premium for the Long strike price or for the Debit Spread premium difference if that strategy is used instead of the Long Call or Put. One example for each of the stocks will be given in their individual sections in this chapter.

The format for computing the individual stock WWI values is the same for each of the 13 stocks as for the OEX. The formula was presented in Chapter 2 and is repeated below:

WWI COMPUTATIONS FOR INDIVIDUAL STOCKS

You should set up a spreadsheet for each stock with the following Columns:

A	B	C	D	E	F
Date	Stock Value	Up	Dn	Up 7 DMA	Dn 7 GMA

G	H	I	J	K
WWI	Up Trigger	Dn Trigger	Cost Dbt Sprd	Prft DbtSprd

The equations to go in these Columns are:

Computation of Up movement = IF((B268 - B267) > 0,B268 - B267,0) = 3.31, where B268 has today's Stock closing value, B267 has yesterday's Stock closing value. IF is the Excel If function.

Computation of Down movement = IF((B268 - B267) < 0,B268 - B267,0), where B268 has today's OEX, B267 has yesterday's OEX. IF is the Excel If function.

UP 7-day Exponential Moving Average = E267 * 0.75 + C268 * 0.25, where E267 is yesterday's **7-day Moving Average,** C268 is today's UP and .75 is the 7-day f2, and .25 is the 7-day f1.

DOWN 7-day Exponential Moving Average = F267 * 0.75 + D268 * 0.25, where F267 is yesterday's 7-day MovAvg, D268 is today's DOWN and .75 is the 7-day f2, and .25 is the 7-day f1.

WWI = 100 * (E268/(E268 - F268)), where E268 is today's UP 7-day MovAvg and F268 is today's DOWN 7-day MovAvg.

The equations in the section above are used for an OEX 2sig covered credit spread and the WWI computation is used for Debit Spread triggers.

Amgen Stock Options

The Amgen spreadsheet has the format for computing WWI shown in the table above. It computes a Put trigger because the WWI is greater than 80. It indicates a Put Debit Spread (Long Put 65 and Short Put 62.5) or a Long Put at 65 would be profitable.

WWI, the Welles-Wilder Indicator, is computed in Column G, the seventh Column to the right, with the equation = 100 * (E8/(E8 - F8)), where cell E8 contains the Up 7-day exponential moving average, and E9 contains the Down 7-day exponential moving average. E8 and E9 mean the cells in Column E in rows 8 and 9. You would need to adjust this number to show the line you are using. Columns H and I to the right of the WWI Column compute when WWI hits the trigger points for a Call Debit Spread (CDS) or a Put Debit Spread (PDS) using the Column H equation, which is: = IF($G8 < 20,5 * ROUND($B8/5,0),"") The Column I equation is given by: = IF($G8 > 80,5 * ROUND($B8/5,0),""). This spreadsheet tells you when to open a *Long Position*.

AMGEN WWI-TRIGGERED LONG CALL POSITION EXAMPLE

A segment of the Amgen spreadsheet is used in which a Long Call is triggered by the WWI < 20 on one day and closing the Long Call position by selling the 10 Long Call at close the next day. Remember, open the positions during the 10-minute grace period after NYSE close until the CBOE options close. This one-day transaction is given below:

* First day: WWI trigger = 13.67 in Column G, Long C computed as 65 in Column H, the cost = $1,500 in Column J.
* Second day: WWI trigger = 53.64 in Column G, Long C no longer indicated in Column H, the value = $2,400 in Column J, *the profit computes = ($2,400 - $1,500) = $900 (before commission)* in Column K

This one-day trade yielded a percent return on cost = 58%, which demonstrates the power of using WWI-triggered Long Options trading using the 13 technical stocks.

The Amgen vs WWI Chart is shown in the figure below for a 6-month segment. This chart should be updated at the beginning of the new Option Month by increasing the stock and WWI row numbers on the curves to be the next expiration date row number. The smooth curve is the 20-day moving average for Amgen. When the WWI gets below 20, the Amgen rises; when WWI goes above 80, then Amgen drops. The lighter triangles show Amgen's movements during the 6-month time period. The darker triangles show the WWI movements during the same period. The chart was printed three days before the next expiration, so the printing date was the last day used for the 20-day moving average, and the information after that was calculated by the moving average extrapolation algorithm.

The moving average line is always right on top of the stock information line at the right-hand end of the charts, where the data is extrapolated. *Please note: the other 12 Stock Charts are similar and will not be repeated here. But you may email the author at jonschl@verizon.net and receive as email attachment the most recent WWI charts for the OEX and 13 Stocks by mailing a $12 check to cover the handling costs. This file is called OEXStlChrts.*

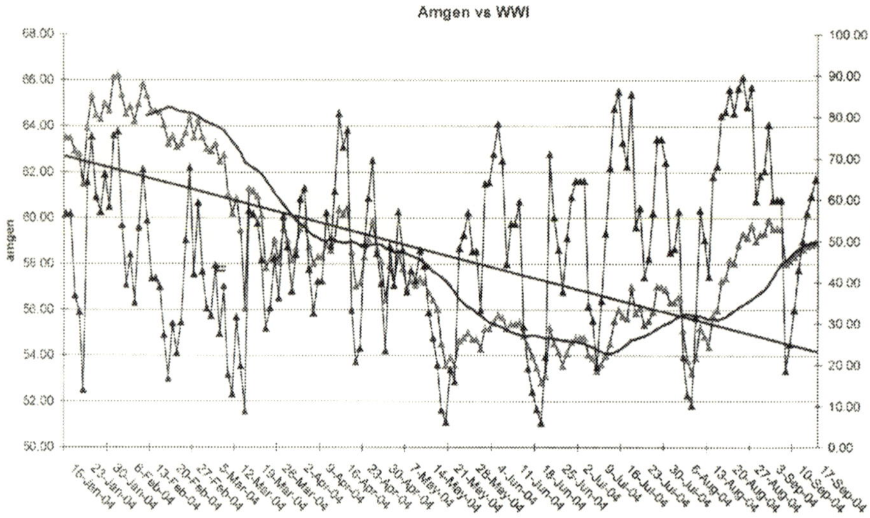
Amgen vs WWI
amgen
WWI

Cisco WWI-Triggered Long Put Position Example

The format for the Cisco spreadsheet uses the common format presented under Amgen for computing WWI and the Long Call or Long Put Triggers and the Cost and Profit for any executed Long Positions.

Scanning the Cisco Spreadsheet one day, I found the WWI = 81.22 triggering a Long Put at strike price 20, having a premium of 1.1, costing $1,100 for 10 options. The next day, Cisco dropped as the WWI predicted and the Put at strike price 20 was closed at a premium of 1.5 with the P20 value at $1,500, which gave a profit before commission of $400 for the one-day trade.

Dell WWI-Triggered Long Put Position Example

The format for the Dell spreadsheet uses the common format presented under Amgen for computing WWI and the Long Call or Long Put Triggers and the Cost and Profit for executed Long Positions.

In the Dell spreadsheet one day, a Long Put 35 at premium 1.05 was triggered by WWI > 80 which cost $1,050 to open and two days later the WWI dropped to 40.86, a signal to close the Long P35 at premium 2.15 at a value of $2,150, yielding a profit of $1,100 - $70 round-trip commission = $1,030. This profitable two-day trade yielded a return on cost of 98.2%:

The WWI signal for this trade came on Thursday, one day before the September options expiration, so October options were used for this trade rather than September options. The rapid decay in premium values at the end of the September options month would have made September options unsuitable. *This 2-trading-day transaction is typical and shows the potential power of the WWI-triggered long positions for stocks.* So WWI triggers of Long positions allow you to add to your monthly profit.

eBay WWI-Triggered Long Call Position Example

The format for the eBay spreadsheet uses the common format presented under Amgen for computing WWI and the Long Call or Long Put Triggers and the Cost and Profit for executed Long Positions.

In the eBay spreadsheet, a Long Call at premium 3.3 was triggered by WWI < 20 which cost $3,300 to open 10 Long Calls at strike price 50. The next day, the WWI rose to 39.42, a signal to close the Long C50 with a premium of 4.2 to yield a value of $4,200 which gave a profit $830 after commission of $70. This profitable one-day trade yielded a return on cost of 25.1%

This example is typical of what can be earned using eBay WWI-triggered Long Calls or Puts. This "target of opportunity" uncovered by WWI adds to the profits of OEX and eBay covered credit spreads. You must understand that among the 13 stocks, usually you will have at least one WWI trigger each month, but if not, don't trade. WWI gives a mathematically sound basis for opening a Long position. The only hazard in Debit Spreads is if the WWI *hangs up* > 80 or *sticks down* < 20 for several days allowing the premium to decay causing a loss instead of a profit.

IBM WWI-Triggered Long Put Position Example

The format for the IBM Spreadsheet uses the common format presented under Amgen for computing WWI and the Long Call or Long Put Triggers and the Cost and Profit for executed Long Positions

Scanning the above spreadsheet, a Long Put 95 was triggered by WWI > 80 which cost $1,800 to open 10 options at premium 1.8. Two days later the WWI dropped to 55.91, a signal to close the Long P95 at a premium of only 1.6, giving a value of $1,600, yielding a *loss* before commission = $200. This two-day trade shows you can lose as well as profit from this strategy.

What happened to cause this loss? I believe it was because an October position was opened on the September expiration day, when the expiration-day premiums were unusually high because of the up-coming new Option Month. So I think you should follow the rule: *Don't make WWI-triggered trades on the last-day of the Option Month.*

Intel WWI-Triggered Long Put Position Example

The format for the Intc spreadsheet uses the common format presented under Amgen for computing WWI and the Long Call or Long Put Triggers and the Cost and Profit for executed Long Positions.

In the intc spreadsheet, a Long Put 30 at premium 1.65 was triggered by WWI > 80 which cost $1,650 to open, and next day the WWI dropped to 58.00, a signal to close the Long P30 at a premium of 1.95 giving a value of $1,950 and yielding a profit after commission of $230. This profitable one-day trade yielded a return on cost of 13.9%.

Microsoft WWI-Triggered Long Put Position Example

The format for the Msft spreadsheet uses the common format presented under Amgen for computing WWI and the Long Call or Long Put Triggers and the Cost and Profit for executed Long Positions.

In the Msft spreadsheet, a Long Put 30 at premium = 0.85 was triggered by WWI > 80 which cost $850 to open 10 Long Puts. The next day, the WWI dropped to 52.07, a signal to close the Long P30 at premium of 0.5, yielding a value of $500, which meant a loss after commission of $420. This one-day loss is another example of opening an October position on September expiration day and the next day, even though the market dropped as the WWI predicted, the closing of the position resulted in a loss.

These two losing WWI examples reinforce the rule: DO NOT open a WWI-triggered long position on the last day of the option month using the new option month for the new position!

QQQQ WWI-Triggered Long Put Position Example

The format for the QQQQ spreadsheet uses the common format presented under Amgen for computing WWI and the Long Call or Long Put Triggers and the Cost and Profit for executed Long Positions.

In the QQQQ spreadsheet, a Long Put 34 at premium of 0.5 was triggered by WWI > 80 which cost $500 to open 10 options. Two days later, the WWI dropped to 32.45 which was a signal to close the Long P34 at a premium of 0.7, giving a value of $700 and yielding for the P34, a profit after commission of $130. This profitable two-day trade yielded a return on cost of 26%. *I have noted that usually several of the 13 stocks have a Put trigger on the same day, meaning there was a general run up of the tech stocks that caused the WWI > 80.*

ORACLE WWI-TRIGGERED LONG PUT POSITION EXAMPLE

The format for the Orcl spreadsheet uses the common format presented under Amgen for computing WWI and the Long Call or Long Put Triggers and the Cost and Profit for executed Long Positions.

A Long Put at strike price 15 and premium 0.4 was triggered by WWI > 80 which cost $400 to open 10 options. Next day, the WWI dropped to 44.74, a signal to close the Long P15 at a premium of 0.65 for a value of $650, yielding a profit before commission of $250, or $180 after commission of $70. Another example of a profitable one-day trade or 45% return on cost.

Similar WWI-triggered Long Call or Put positions could have been given for the other four stocks, but will not be presented here since the examples show the power of this strategy. Remember: Buy ATM Calls when WWI < 20 & Buy ATM Puts when WWI > 80. Close the position when a profit would result within three days. Close the position with a small loss if the position does not result in a profit after three days—or apply the TRIAD rule.

In the Examples presented above for WWI-triggered Long Calls or Puts, how many were profitable and what were the overall results?

* The Total Cost for the 9 Trades = $12,500 or an average cost = $1,389
* The Total Profit for the 9 Trades = $3,070 after commission or an average profit = $341
* The Average # days for the 9 Trades = 1.33 or an average daily profit = $256
* There were 7 winning trades and 2 losing trades or 77% winning trades.
* The average return on Cost of 24.6%

Note: all trades were profitable except those opened on Expiration Friday for the next Option Month!

2 Sigma Computations for the 13 Stocks Options

The 2 sigma computations can be computed in your spreadsheets for each of the 13 stocks using the Excel standard deviation function (STDEV). The 2 sigma is a measure of the stocks' volatility. Using 2 sigma covered spreads is too risky, however, because of large jumps or drops that can occur in the individual stock prices when adverse or positive market information occurs. Early in this chapter I presented two examples of 2 sigma covered spreads for eBay and QQQQ which were profitable, so for those of you who want to take the risk, this 2 sigma covered spread can be used.

Some typical 2 sigma values are presented below, but you should compute the up-to-date values. I extracted these values from my SelfAdapStkOp workbook in the sector of the worksheet that computes 2 sigmas. Listed below is a snapshot of 13-month 2 sigmas for OEX and the 13 stocks so you may compare what all of the values were at the same time:

1. OEX: Call 2sig = 25.01, Put 2sig = 24.60
2. Amgen: Call 2sig = 7.09, Put 2sig = 8.92
3. Cisco : Call 2sig = 3.83, Put 2sig = 3.54
4. Dell: Call 2sig = 2.54, Put 2sig = 4.05
5. DNA: Call 2sig = 8.22, Put 2sig = 6.57
6. eBay: Call 2sig = 11.85, Put 2sig = 9.66
7. IBM: Call 2sig = 8.05, Put 2sig = 5.85
8. Intc: Call 2sig = 4.15, Put 2sig = 4.37
9. Msft: Call 2sig = 2.85, Put 2sig = 3.45
10. Nflx: Call 2sig = 7.03, Put 2sig = 7.29
11. QQQQ: Call 2sig = 3.08, Put 2sig = 3.35
12. Orcl: Call 2sig = 1.89, Put 2sig = 1.42
13. Sina: Call 2sig = 7.81, Put 2sig = 13.55
14. Yahoo: Call 2sig = 4.76, Put 2sig = 4.88

Another use for the Call and Put 2 sigma computations is to compare the probability of a rise or drop in one of the underlying stocks. For example, the eBay Call 2 sigma is greater than the Put 2 sigma, so the eBay is more likely to rise than fall.

Your stock spreadsheets must be updated monthly for the 2 sigma computations using the 2 sigma calculation equation = 2 * STDEV(L3:L15) for the Call 2 sigma and = 2 * STDEV(M3:M15) for the Put 2 sigma, where the Ls are the Ups and the Ms are the downs for the last 13 months. The update means increasing the L3:L15 to L4:L16 for the Call and M3:M15 to M4:M16 for the Put. This maintains 13 months for the 2 sigma computations. In other words, we are using the last 13 months MAX and MIN variations to compute the Call and Put 2sig.

Naked 2 Sigma Spreads or Short Calls or Puts for Stock Options

The 2 sigma Naked Credit Spread Strategy for OEX was described in Chapter 4 as a means for generating more initial credit than the Covered Credit Spread, but it is unsuitable for many traders because the SEC requires a minimum Margin of $50,000 for the OEX. So until your trading capital exceeds $50,000, this strategy cannot be used for OEX. However, it is a feasible strategy for use in Stock Options since the minimum Margin is 10% of the Stock Price.

For example, if eBay = 83, the minimum Margin per option is computed as = 0.1 * 83 * 100 = $830 or for 10 Short eBay Calls or Put would require $8,300. Or for 10 Naked eBay Spreads the margin = 2 * 10 * 8.30 = $16,600. Note that the 100 is the number of dollars per point for stock options. *So we may add the 2 sigma Short Calls or Puts and Naked 2sigma Spreads to our list of strategies to consider for Stock Options because the modest minimum Margin is low compared to the Minimum $50,000 required for OEX Naked Spreads.*

One advantage of using the Growth stocks is that a Put Credit Spread or Short Put can be used with the short strike price closer to the market resulting in a larger Initial Credit than for a 2 sigma Short Put. The theory is that growth stocks go up instead of down. I got this idea from Jerry of B&J Options Brokers who uses near-the-market naked Puts for growth stocks to generate good profits.

Here is an example of my spread strategy using a January Intel Put Credit Spread: I opened 10 Intel Jan Put Credit Spreads: Short P30 and Long P27.5 (designated as P30/27.5) for a value of 0.45 which yielded an Initial Credit = 10 * 100 * 0.45 –74 commission = $376 and with Intel = 31.11, two trading days after the opening of the Jan Option Month. At the third Friday options expiration, Intel closed at 32.89, meaning the P30/27.5 spread was now worthless. So the $376 I had received as initial credit became a profit of $376. The margin for this trade = 10 * 100 * 2.5 = $2,500. This trade gave a return on Margin = 15.0% = 180% annualized return.

How does the 2 sigma Naked Credit Spread work for Stock Options?

The 2 sigma Call and Put strike prices are computed as shown in the Intel Put Covered Credit Spread example given above. Then, to open 10 naked credit spreads, you sell 10 of the 2sig Short Calls and sell 10 of the 2sig Short Puts. *Initial Credit = 10 * (Call premium + Put premium) * 100 - commission.*

Please note there are 2 algorithms for computing the naked spread Margins:

1. The simple one of computing 10% of the stock price, or the equation Margin1 = 0.1 * StkPr * 100 * NOPs, where 0.1 is the 10% factor, StkPr is the current value of the stock in dollars, 100 is the number of dollars per point for options, and NOPs is the number of options
2. A second algorithm that must be computed and compared with the first is given by the equation Margin2 = 0.2 * (StkPr + CallPrm - CallOTM) * 100 * NOPS, where CallPrm is the value of the Call Premium in points, CallOTM is the number of points the Call is "out-of-the-money" which is the number of points the Call is above the current market value.
3. The margin applicable to the naked spread = MAX (Margin1, Margin2), i.e. the greatest!

The algorithms appear more complex than they really are. We'll use eBay as an example, to show how to compute the margin on 10 naked spreads with the following parameters:

* eBay = 56.5 and the 2sig Short Call = 62.5 with a premium of 0.4, then the Call Initial Credit = 10 * 100 * 0.4 – Comm = $400 - $50 = $350.
* The Call Margin1= 0.1 * 62.5 * 100 * 10 = $6,250
* The Call Margin2 = 10 * 100 * .2 * (62.5 + 0.4 - 6) = $11,250
* The Call Margin = MAX ($6250, $11250) = $11,250
* For the Put Side: 2sig Short Put = 52.5 with a premium of .45, then
* The Put Initial Credit = 10 * 100 * 0.450 - 50Comm = $400.
* The Put Margin1 = 0.1 * 62.5 * 100 * 10 = $6,250
* The Put Margin2 = 10 * 100 * .2 * (52.5 + 0.45 - 4.0) = $9,790
* The Put Margin = MAX($9790,$6250) = $9,790

The rule is the *worst case* of the margin1 and Margin2 applies for *both* the Put side and Call side of the naked spread.

When trading on the Chicago exchange the, total Margin = Call Margin + Put Margin = $21,040

When trading on the London exchange, the worst case of the Call or Put Margin would be applied, or in this eBay example, the Trading Margin = $11,250. The rationale for London using only the worst case is that a double-sided Margin can only lose on one side, not both sides. *I'm not sure what the rationale is for the Chicago rule!*

Naked Stock Options Spreads sounds like a good strategy, what are the problems?

1. Often there are not 2sig Calls or Puts for the stock of interest.
2. In other cases the 2sig premiums are so small that the Commission is greater than the Initial Credit before commission. However, these problems can be overcome by using the near-to-the-market Put Credit Spread (*nearer than 2 sigma below the market*). The near-to-the-market strike prices are almost always available. They are traded with high volume and are a good way to make good return on your risk capital. *Please note, however, that such Put Credit Spreads are more risky than the spreads with the Short Puts 2 sigma below the market.*

Nine of the 13 Stocks Were Surveyed for Possible 2sig Naked Credit Spreads for the October Options Month in the section below using data from the SelfAdapStkOp software package and using the segment of the worksheets, where the 2 sigma and the Short Call and Put Strike Prices are computed. The stock price data and the stock option data for the October options month were taken at close on expiration day for the September options month.

The margin equations for Stock Options use the same algorithms as in the eBay naked spread example given above. The Call and Put Initial Credit Equation formats are also the same and will not be repeated below. Both the Call and Put 13 month 2 sigma computations are performed in each stock's spreadsheet section, where the 2 sigmas are computed for covered spreads (that use Calls and Puts and the next higher Call strike price and next lower Put strike price). The naked spread Margins only use one Call position and one Put position. For several of the nine stocks listed below, only one side of the naked spread was available, which was really just a Short Call or Short Put position.

Please note: if the covered credit spread rather than the naked credit spread were used, the margins would be half as much. Covered Spread Margins use the common algorithm given here: Call CCSS Margin = NOPs * 100 * CallSprdWdth, where NOPs = number of options, 100 = $s /pt. Call SprdWdth = spread width in points, Put CCSS Margin = NOPs * 100 * PutSprdWdth

Listing of 2 Sigma Naked Spread Computations for Nine Stock Options

Amgen 2sig Naked Spread

Amgen had an excellent two-sided naked spread. For a $8,312 Margin (London Rule) you received $360 initial credit for % return on Margin of 4.09% for the month, annualized = 49.0%. Using the Chicago Rule, this return would be halved since the margin is doubled.

It looks good, but how safe is the position? Nine trading days into the October options month, the Amgen = 66.15, 6.35 below the Short C72.5 and 1.15 above the Short P65. So if Amgen didn't drop below or rise above 72.5 on October expiration, then the initial credit would become profit. *What happened?* Amgen closed at 63.01 on expiration day, making the $360 profit.

Cisco 2SIG Short Call

Cisco had no two-sided naked spread. The Call side had a premium of only .05, not enough to pay the $70 commission, and the Put side had no position. This often happens for low-priced stocks such as Cisco. However, Cisco was a good candidate for a close-to-the-market Put Credit Spread.

Dell 2SIG Short Put

Dell had no Call side naked spread and a Put side naked spread of only 0.25 which had an initial credit of only $80 after commission of $70. The Put Margin was $4,587, yielding a return of 1.74% Initial Credit to Margin. *However, Dell was a good candidate for a close -to-the-market Put Credit Spread which would have yielded more initial credit.*

How safe is the position? Nine trading days into the October options month, Dell = 33.87, 1.37 above the Short P32.5. So if Dell doesn't drop below 32.5 before Oct expiration, then the initial credit becomes profit. *What happened?* On the October expiration day, Dell finished at 36.41, below the Short Call and above the Short Put, making the initial credit into profit. *Note that a P35/32.5 would have finished safe giving more profit for less Margin.*

eBay 2SIG Short Put

eBay had no Short Call position, but had a 2sig Short Put 50 with a premium of 0.7 which yielded an initial credit of $330 after commission of $70. The minimum Margin $5732, so the initial credit had a return of 5.76%.

This 2sig Short Put appears potentially profitable, but how safe is the position? Nine trading days into the Oct OpMo the eBay = 55.10, 5.1 above the Short P50. So if eBay doesn't drop below 50 before Oct expiration, then the initial credit of $330 becomes profit.

IBM 2sig Naked Spread

IBM had a two-sided naked spread at short C100 and short P85 for an Initial Credit = $860. For a worst case Margin of $12,456 you would have received $860 initial credit, at 3.29% return on Margin using London rules, half that return using Chicago rules.

It looks good, but how safe is the position? Nine trading days into the Oct OpMo the IBM = 90.08, 9.92 below the Short C100 and 5.08 above the Short P85. So if IBM doesn't drop below 85 or rise above 100 before Oct expiration, then the initial credit of $860 becomes profit. Remember the 2sig spread theory sets the probability of winning at 95%, but you will lose 5% of the time. One advantage of the Naked Short Spread is that if the Short Call or Short Put is threatened, you can close out the threatened Short Call or Put and re-open the position at a safe strike price, usually with a net profit. Such corrective moves for the Covered Credit Spreads almost always result in a loss for the month.

Intel 2sig Naked Spread

Intel had a two-sided naked spread at Short C32.5 and Short Put 27.5. The worst case Margin of $4,112 Margin (London rules) gave you a two-sided initial credit = $310 for a return on Margin of 7.54%. Using Chicago rules the return is halved.

A good return on opening the position at the beginning of the Oct Option Month, but how safe is the position? Nine trading days into the Oct OpMo, Intel = 28.62, almost 4 below the Short C32.5 and over 1 above the Short P27.5. So if Intel doesn't drop below 27.5 or rise above 32.5 before Oct expiration, then the initial credit of $335 becomes profit.

Microsoft 2sig Naked Spread

Microsoft had no 2 sigma two-sided naked spread positions available.

QQQQ 2sig Naked Spread

QQQQ had a two-sided naked spread, Short Call at 36 and Short Put at 32 for a net Initial Credit of $210. Still the return on Margin of $9216 is 2.28% (London rules). Half that return using Chicago rules.

How safe is the position? Nine trading days into the Oct OpMo the QQQQ = 33.23, 3.77 below the Short C37. So if QQQQ doesn't move above 36 or below 32 before Oct then the initial credit of $210 becomes profit.

Oracle 2sig Naked Spread

Oracle had no 2 sigma positions available—neither a Short Call nor a Short Put. Oracle is the lowest priced stock of the nine stocks included in this survey, which means often it doesn't have 2 sigma positions available. So it appears you will have to stick with the WWI-triggered Debit Spreads for Oracle or else use the riskier close-to-the-market Short Puts, depending on a continued rise in the price.

Conclusions: For the Stock Naked Spreads for the nine stock examples, the highest Margin was for IBM which had a Margin of $12,456 in the example for the October Options Month when the IBM stock price = 91.18, the highest price of the nine stocks which caused the highest Margin.

Results of Year's Paper Trading for 13 Stock Options Using Welles-Wilder Indicator (WWI) Triggers

A one-year survey was made of the trading results of the 13 stock options in this chapter compared with OEX and using the WWI trigger to either buy or sell 10 options with strike prices at-the-money (ATM). In the case of the 13 stocks, the Long Position was the most profitable. The three best profit results for the Long Positions for Stock Options were for eBay, Amgen, and Microsoft in that order. For the OEX, the best position was a Debit Spread Position which made almost $7,000 profit.

In each case it was assumed that 10 Options were used, the following rules were used:

1. If the WWI *hangs up* above 80 for three days,
   close and take a small loss.
2. If the WWI *sticks down* below 20 for three days,
   close and take a small loss.
3. When a Long Call or Put makes a profit,
   close the position with even a small profit. *Don't wait and hope for more,* in other words: *don't be greedy!*
4. Avoid opening a WWI-triggered Long Call or Put on expiration day or the Thursday before, because a *Chaos Pattern* I observed is that a profit doesn't occur even when the market moves in the direction which would ordinarily make a profit, because of the decay in options premiums at the end of the options month. If you want to open a Long Position near the Expiration Friday, you should use the *next* options month, rather than the expiring month.

FIVE-YEAR CAPITAL GROWTH MODEL FOR STOCK OPTIONS TRADING

We now have three strategies to use for trading Stock Options.

1. 2sig Covered Credit Spreads,
2. WWI-triggered ATM Long Calls or Puts or Debit Spreads
3. 2sig Naked Credit Spreads or Short Calls or Short Puts.

The advantage of the Stock Options Trading is that you can start with a modest initial Capital of 25,000 and make your Capital grow significantly year by year. I made a simplistic Stock Generation model, generated using Excel, which assumes that eBay will be used for a monthly 2 sigma Covered Credit Spreads to generate a monthly income augmented by WWI-triggered Long Call or Long Put positions. The Model assumes you have an initial capital of $25,000 and your stock option profits make this initial capital grow. It begins in Oct 03 and goes to Sept 08, a period of five years and provides a return on capital of 372% for five years or an annual capital growth of 74.5%. This model is not achievable since it shows no monthly losses. Over a period of five years, there will be some monthly losses. I have used modest monthly profit points to compensate for not including losses in the model. But another valuable use for the model is to use it as an accounting tool to keep track of your actual trading results.

SUMMARY

The chapter shows how to do the computations needed for profitable Stock Options trading using Excel workbooks which you can create using the equations provided in this book. The equations used are given so you can create your own Excel-based trading software if you wish. The **2 sigma Stock Covered Credit Spread** or the **2 sigma Naked Credit Spread** provide a means for generating income for Stock Options *but it is a risky strategy because news announcements can cause large movements in single stocks*. It is better to use **Long Calls or Puts** triggered by the **WWI** for the stocks covered in this chapter. Remember:

1. **WWI > 80** triggers a **Long Put** position.
2. **WWI < 20** triggers a **Long Call** position.

I recommend you do *paper* trading for a month or two; tracking the stocks daily; making the *paper* trades; getting a feel for how the strategies work in practice. After you feel confident, then you can switch to real trading. I wish you good fortune in using the Stock Options Strategies described in this chapter and automated by an Excel workbook. My workbook SelfAdapStkOp is a possible tool for computing the parameters for trading. This workbook can be ordered by email from jonsch1@verizon.com. Any workbook so ordered will be sent to you by email attachment. You may also wish to visit the author's website at http://www.jonschilleroptions.com/.

CHAPTER 6

COMMODITY FUTURE OPTIONS

For a number of years the readers of my first two options books asked me why I didn't write a book about Commodity Future Options. At that time I was living in Spain trading OEX and SEI (the London American style options based on the FTSE-100 Index). I investigated the websites for finding realtime or near realtime Commodity Future Prices as the basis for Future Options prices. I decided at that time that the 2sig Future Options Covered Credit Spread Strategy was not suitable for trading because most Futures don't have monthly expiration dates.

One of my basic rules is to always use the current Options Month for CCSS, so that at the end of four or five weeks the CCSS becomes worthless converting the Initial Credit into Profit. Instead most Future Options expire every other month or quarterly. That's why the television financial announcers often refer to the quarterly Options Expiration date in December, March, June, and September as the **triple witching hour** (when Future Options, Stock Options and Index Options expire on the same-day). These quarterly expiration third Fridays are very busy trading days.

After I returned to California in late 2001, I began researching the use of Debit Spreads for my familiar OEX Index Options trading. The Debit Spreads are triggered by the WWI and provide excellent short-term profits. I investigated the use of Future Options that utilized WWI-triggered Debit Spreads and found it worked well. The Debit Spreads can be used successfully for Future Options in out-months with options expirations later than the current Options Month when there is good volume. I began paper trading the 10 Future Options listed in Chapter 1 and tabulated below in this Chapter. As a result of this trading, I came up with two rules:

1. Debit Spreads triggered by WWI is the best strategy to use for Future Options.
2. 2Sig Credit Spreads can be used, but this strategy is complicated by the fact that there are not monthly expirations for most of the Future Options.

I found that Future Options using WWI-triggered Debit Spreads was a reliable method of generating short-term profits.

* **When WWI > 80, open a Put Debit Spread.** This is a signal that the market is going to drop. To open, buy ATM Put Options and sell the same number at the next strike price lower. The Put Debit Spread costs less than a Long ATM Put because the Short Put is at a lower strike price.
* **When WWI < 20, open a Call Debit Spread.** This is a signal that the market is going to rise. To open, buy ATM Call Options and sell the same number at the next strike price higher. The Call Debit Spread costs less than a Long ATM Call because the Short Call is at a higher strike price.

Since my earlier OEX software, called Oexstrgy, had the algorithms for computing the 7-day Welles-Wilder Indicator (WWI) for the OEX, it was easy to adapt my new software, SelfAdapFutOp, to compute the WWI for the Future Options.

The WWI as a Trigger to Open Call or Put Debit Spreads.

Since the Debit Spread Strategy (DSS) is well suited for out-month options as well as current-month options, it was well suited to Future Options which do not have current-month options many times during the trading year. I had all the tools for Future Options trading except one: the historical data to do paper trading to validate my DSS strategy before doing my first real trade. I began entering the Futures Closing prices for the 10 Commodity Future Options selected for my new SelfAdapFutOp spreadsheets.

Since I use the 7-day Exponential Moving Average, which needs only two days of data (today's and yesterday's), I could begin computing WWI immediately. I found using the WWI-triggered Debit Spreads for the 10 Commodity Future Options listed in Chapter 1 and described in this chapter was an excellent way to trade. These 10 futures have been selected from a large number of futures as being suitable for trading their options. These 10 futures are tracked in my Self-Adaptive Future Options Software which computes the WWI and the Call or Put ATM Strike Price when WWI < 20 or WWI > 80. Details of the logic equations utilized to display the triggered strike price are described in this chapter in the section about the Common Format Spreadsheets.

I did research into the possibility of using the 2sig Covered Credit Spread or the 2sig Naked Credit Spread that worked so well for OEX Options in Chapter 4, but in many cases the Future Options were not suitable for either of these Credit Spread strategies for the simple reason that there was no options expiration in the current options month. Another peculiarity is that the underlying Futures expiration month and the Options expiration month were not identical. This is not usually a problem for Debit Spreads, since the Future Prices for different future expiration dates track each other with only a few points difference.

I will give examples of Debit Spreads triggered by WWI. Then I will present the 2sig Covered Spread Strategy for each of the 10 Future Options using Orion Website Futures Options data for the next expiration which was generally about 40 to 45 days. *I prefer to use Debit Spreads, but for those of you who are enterprising and want to try Credit Spreads, the potential results are presented for your perusal.*

KEY PARAMETERS FOR THE 10 FUTURE OPTIONS

The 10 Future Options work well using the WWI-triggered Call or Put Debit Spread Strategy. The fact that many Futures Options do not have monthly expirations is no obstacle for trading Debit Spreads, since the *next* Option Month normally has the highest options volume. The list below displays the Call and Put 2 sigmas for 13 months as well as one Internet Future Options broker's Margins required to open a Future Options Position.

Future	Commodity	Exchange	MinMrgnRqd	C2Sig	P2sig
1. Kansas Wheat	KW	KCBT	$812	45.63	32.97
2. Corn	C	CBOT	$540	30.08	31.50
3. Soybeans	S	CBOT	$945	111.0	148.05
4. Coffee	KC	NYBOT	$2,100	7.70	6.00
5. Gold	GC	NYMEX	$2,025	23.87	20.49
6. Crude Oil	CL	NYMEX	$4,050	3.69	4.47
7. SPX futures	SP	CME	$17,813	25.90	50.49
8. US Bonds	US	CBOT	$3,000	6.16	6.77
9. 10-Year Notes	TY	CBOT	$3,000	4.24	4.31
10.Yen Futures	JY	CME	$2,160	0.0403	0.0448

The margin requirements list above is very important since it tells how much Margin (cash) you need in your account to trade different future options. The margin is much less than the cost of a position. For example, the US Bonds usually cost around $50,000 to open a Debit Spread, yet the margin is only $3,000. The SPX (S&P) 500 Future options usually cost about $2,500 for a Debit Spread, yet the margin is $17,813

The list below shows the relevant factors needed to trade WWI-triggered Debit Spreads for the selected Future Options. Cost and Profit figures are typical; actual cost and profit figures will be given for specific examples later in this chapter.

Future	$/Point	#OPS	CstDbtSprd$	TypPrft	%Ret
1. Kansas Wheat	$50	10	$2,500	$625	25%
2. Corn	$50	10	$1,500	$375	25%
3. Soybeans	$50	10	$5,000	$313	6.25%
4. Coffee	$375	10	$5,325	$666	12.5%
5. Gold	$100	10	$4,200	$1,050	25%
6. Crude Oil	$1,000	10	$2,300	$575	25%
7. SPX futures	$250	4	$2,600	$650	25%
8. US Bonds	$100,000	1	$50,000	$12,500	25%
9. 10YrTrsNotes	$100,000	1	$40,650	$10,156	25%
10. Yen Futures	$1,250	10	$5,375	$1344	25%

As you may see, the dollars per point vary from $50 for the three Commodity Future Options to $100,000 per point for the two US Financial Future Options. Also, the expiration dates are bi-monthly or quarterly, depending on the Future. My favorite website for Futures and Futures Option data is **www.orionfutures.com** and provides all active traders the data needed to trade.

The table shows the number of options to use in the Debit Spread to keep the Cost of the Spread between $1,500 to $6,000. However, the Debit Spread Cost for the US Bond and US 10-Year Note Options is typically $40,000 to $50,000 because the dollars per point are so high = $100,000. The profit potential for these US financial Futures is high; you need a Margin of $3,000 in your trading account before you can try these two Options. *Using my rule: Never use more than 50% of your Trading Capital for either Debit Spread Cost or Credit Spread Margin.*

These future options can also be used for 2sig Covered Credit Spreads, but some do not have monthly expirations, which means they cannot be used each month.

COMMON FORMAT FOR THE 10 EXCEL SPREADSHEETS

A	B	C	D	E	F
Date	Future	Up	Dn	7DMAup	7DMAdn

G	H	I	J	K	L
WWI	Ctrig	PTrig	CST	PRFT	DBTSPD

Column A has the date for each trading-day.

Column B has the underlying market name—for example, corn, soybeans, coffee, gold, etc.—for its title. You need to put the closing value of the future in the cells at the end of the trading day.

Column C computes the market movement in the up direction using the equation: = IF((B7 - B6) > 0,B7 - B6,0)

Column D computes the market movement in the down direction using the equation: = IF((B7 - B6) < 0,B7 - B6,0)

Column E computes the Up 7-day exponential moving average using the equation: = E6 * 0.75 + C7 * 0.25

Column F computes the Down 7-day exponential moving average using the equation: = F6 * 0.75 + D7 * 0.25

Column G computes the Welles-Wilder Indicator using the equation: = 100 * (E7/(E7 - F7))

Column H computes Call Strike Price if the WWI < 20 using the equation: = IF($G7 < 20,5 * ROUND($B7/5,0),"")

The Columns H and I in the spreadsheets are for signaling when WWI is triggered as a potentially profitable Debit Spread position. The Future Options Strike Price for the ATM Long Call is computed in Column H and the ATM Long Put is computed in Column I.

Column I computes the Put Strike Price if the WWI > 80 using the equation: = IF($G7 > 80,5 * ROUND($B7/5,0),"")

Column J computes the cost of any triggered Call or Put Debit Spread using the equation: Cost = #Ops * $/point * (Premium of Long Option – Premium of Short Option) + Commission.

The Column J can be used for computing the cost of opening the Debit Spread and Column K can be used for computing the short-term profit (or loss) of these short-term positions which are normally open for a few trading days.

Column K computes the profit (or loss) of any Debit Spread opened or closed using the equation: Profit = Value of Debit Spread on day opened – Value of Debit Spread on day closed

Column L is used to annotate the strike prices of the Long and Short Call or Put Debit Spread and the Option Month for the expiration of the Future Options.

Notes:

1. The row number 7 in the above formulas shows the row number of the date for the day of the computation.
2. The row number 6 in the above formulas depend on the row number of the date for the trading day before the day of the computation.
3. In order to simplify the date algorithm, holidays are included if they fall Monday through Friday and the market value displayed in Column B is set equal to the previous market day's value.

Standard Deviation Computations

The 2 Standard Deviation (2 sig) Computations are computed in a special section of the Futures spreadsheets Columns (M and N) and use exactly the same format and Excel formulas as do the computations for OEX and the 13 Tech Stocks shown in Chapter 5. I don't recommend using 2sig Covered Credit Spreads for the Future Options, except for the S&P 500 Future Options. *If you do use Credit Spreads for Future Options, be sure you pick ones with the Current Option Month for Expiration. Don't Use Out-Month Expirations which are too risky.*

Short Call = 5 * ROUND((B247 + M22)/5,0), where B247 contains the Future value at Options expiration date and M22 contains the value of the Call 2 sigma computed with the equation: =2 * STDEV(M9:M21), where the space from M9 to M21 contains the maximum variation of the underlying Future for the last 13 options months.

Long Call = M22 + 5, where M22 contains the strike price of the Short Call and 5 is the next higher Call strike price.

Short Put = 5 * ROUND((B247 - N22)/5,0), where B247 contains the Future value at Options expiration date and N22 contains the value of the Put 2 sigma computed with the equation: =2 * STDEV(N9:N21), where the space from N9 to N21 contains the minimum variation of the underlying Future for the last 13 options months.

Long Put = N22 - 5, where N22 contains the strike price of the Short Put and 5 is the next lower Put strike price.

Note: For Future Options that have strike prices closer or wider spaced than 5 points, the 5 would be adjusted accordingly. For example, for US Bonds which have strike prices 1 point apart, a strike price one lower would be used for the Short Put.

A Capital Growth model for Future Options trading is discussed near the end of this chapter. This model shows that if you start with a beginning capital of $25,000, at the end of five years your capital would have grown to $302,078.

How to Use the Common Format Spreadsheets

The common format was shown on above. Each day you should enter the closing market values of the 10 Futures. The other numbers will be calculated automatically. You need to put values in Columns J and K if you open or close a triggered Long or Debit Spread.

TARGETS OF OPPORTUNITY: WWI > 80 OR WWI < 20

You should scan your 10 Future spreadsheets daily seeking the WWI triggers which are indicated in the Columns H for WWI < 20 or Column I for WWI > 80 triggering a potentially profitable Call or Put Debit Spread or Long Call or Put. If you decide to open such a position, the Long Call or Put would be at-the-money, or the strike prices closest to the market. The spreadsheets for all 10 futures have identical formats so the triggers are always shown in Columns H and I just to the right of Column G which computes the WWI. The equation for computing the cost of opening 10 Long Calls or Puts is the same as for the three grain future options: = 10 * 1.05 * 50, where 10 is the number of options, 50 is the $ per point, and 1.05 is the premium difference for the Debit Spread

WWI is computed in Column G, the seventh column to the right, with the equation = 100 * (E8/(E8 - F8)), where cell E8 contains the Up 7-day exponential moving average, and E9 contains the Down 7-day exponential moving average. Columns H and I to the right of the WWI Column compute when WWI hits the trigger points for a Call Debit Spread (Cds) or a Put Debit Spread (Pds) using the Column H equation = IF($G8 < 20,5 * ROUND($B8/5,0),"") and the Column I equation is given by = IF($G8 > 80,5 * ROUND($B8/5,0),""). So this spreadsheet tells you when to open a *Debit Spread.*

KWHEAT FUTURE OPTIONS WWI-TRIGGERED DEBIT SPREAD POSITION

A segment of the Kwheat spreadsheet is used in which a Long Call is triggered by the WWI < 20 on one day and in which the Long Call position is closed by selling the 10 Long Calls at close the next day. This one-day transaction is given below:

* 1st day: WWI trigger = 14.5 in Column G, Long C computed as 350 in Column H, the short C360, the cost = $3776 in Column J for the C350/360 Debit Spread.
* 2nd day: WWI trigger = 62.59 in Column G, Long C no longer indicated in Column H, the value = $4,026 in Column J, *the profit computes = (4,026 - 3,776) = $250 (before commission)* in Column K. This 2-day trade yielded a % return on cost = 6.6%

The Kansas Wheat vs WWI Chart is shown in the figure below. The other Future vs WWI charts are similar and will not be repeated.

The smooth curve in the chart below is the 20-day moving average for Kwheat. The dark horizontal line is the Linear Trend Line. The dark diamonds are WWI positions each day and the lighter squares are the Kwheat values each day. Please note that when the WWI gets below 20, the Kwheat rises and when WWI goes above 80, then Kwheat drops.

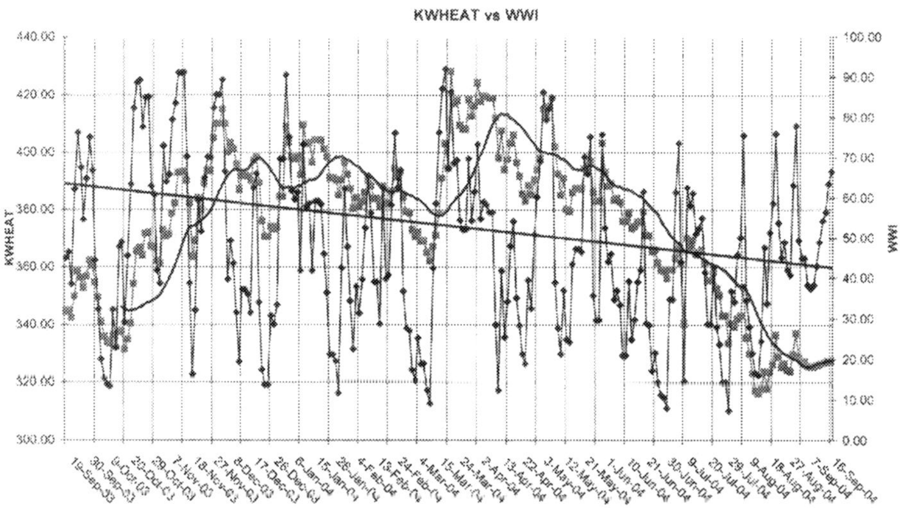

Corn Future Options WWI-Triggered Debit Spread Position

A segment of the Corn spreadsheet is used in which a Long Call is triggered by the WWI <20 on one day and is closed by selling the 10 Long Calls at close the next day. This one-day transaction is given below:

* 1st day: WWI trigger = 14.5 in Column G, Long C computed as 350 in Column H, the short C360, the cost = $3,776 in Column J for the C350/360 Debit Spread.
* 2nd day: WWI trigger = 62.59 in Column G, Long C no longer indicated in Column H, the value = $4,026 in Column J, *the profit computes = (4,026 - 3,776) = $250 (before commission)* in Column K. This was a September spread executed during the July Option Month. This 2-day trade yielded a % return on cost = 6.6%

Soybean Future Options WWI-Triggered Debit Spread Position

A segment of the Soybean spreadsheet is used in which a Put Debit Spread is triggered by the WWI > 80 when the spread was opened by Buying 10 P940 and Selling 10 P920 for a computed Cost = N * $/Pt * PremDel = 10 * 50 * 16 = $8,000, where N = number of options, $/Pt = dollars per point for Soybeans, and PremDel = the difference between the Long Premium and the Short Premium. Two days later the WWI dropped to 56 so the position was closed by selling the 10 Long P940s and buying the 10 Short P920s at close that day. The Premium Difference at Close = 18.4, making the new value of the Debit Spread = 10 * 50 * 18.4 = $9,200. So the Profit computed in Column K = $9,200 - 8,000 = $1,200 - Comm. This 2-day transaction yielded a % return on cost = 1,200/8,000 = 15%.

COFFEE FUTURE OPTIONS WWI-TRIGGERED DEBIT SPREAD POSITION

A segment of the Coffee spreadsheet is used in which a Call Debit Spread is triggered by the WWI < 20 at 13.02 when the spread was opened by Buying 10 C725 and Selling 10 C750 for a computed Cost = N * $/Pt * PremDel = 5 * 375 * 0.7 = $1,313, where N = number of options, $/Pt = dollars per point for Coffee, and PremDel = the difference between the Long Premium and the Short Premium. Three days later the WWI rose to 46 so the position was closed by selling the 10 Long C725 and buying the 10 Short C750 at close. The Premium Difference at Close = 1.56, making the new value of the Debit Spread = 5 * 375 * 1.56 = $2925. So the Profit computed in Column K = $2,925 - 1,313 = $1,613 - Comm. This 3-day transaction yielded a % return on cost = 1,613/1,313 = 122.8%.

GOLD FUTURE OPTIONS WWI-TRIGGERED DEBIT SPREAD POSITION

A segment of the Gold spreadsheet is used in which a Put Debit Spread is triggered by the WWI > 80 and the spread was opened by Buying 10 P405 and Selling 10 P400 for a computed Cost = N * $/Pt * PremDel = 10 * 100 * 0.4= $400, where N = number of options, $/Pt = dollars per point for Gold, and PremDel = the difference between the Long Premium and the Short Premium. Two days later the WWI dropped to 68.25 so the position was closed by selling the 10 Long P405 and buying the 10 Short P400 at close the next day. The Premium Difference at Close = 0.6, making the new value of the Debit Spread = 10 * 50 * 18.4 = $600. So the Profit computed in Column K = $600 - 400 = $200 - Comm. This 2-day transaction yielded a % return on cost = 200/400 = 50%.

Crude Oil Future Options WWI-Triggered Debit Spread Position

A segment of the Crude Oil spreadsheet is used in which a Put Debit Spread is triggered by the WWI > 80 when the spread was opened by Buying 10 P41.50 and Selling 10 P41.00 for a computed Cost = N * $/Pt * PremDel = 10 * 1,000 * 0.11 = $1,100, where N = number of options, $/Pt = dollars per point for oil, and PremDel = the difference between the Long Premium and the Short Premium. Two days later the WWI dropped to 43.43 so the position was closed by selling the 10 Long P41.50 and buying the 10 Short P41.00 at close the next day. The Premium Difference at Close = 0.3, making the new value of the Debit Spread = 10 * 1,000 * 0.3 = $3,000. So the Profit computed in Column K = $3,000 - $1,100 = $2,900 - Comm. This 2-day transaction yielded a % return on cost = 2,900/400 = 725%.

SPX Future Options WWI-Triggered Debit Spread Position

A segment of the SPX Futures spreadsheet is used in which a Call Debit Spread is triggered by the WWI < 20 and the spread was opened by Buying 4 C1115 and Selling 4 C1120 for a computed Cost = N * $/Pt * PremDel = 4 * 250 * 1.4= $1400, where N = number of options, $/Pt = dollars per point for SPX Futures, and PremDel = the difference between the Long Premium and the Short Premium. Three days later the WWI went up to 26.75 so the position was closed by selling the 4 Long C1115 and buying the 4 Short C1120 at close the next day. The Premium Difference at Close = 5, making the new value of the Debit Spread = 4 * 250 * 5 = $5,000. So the Profit computed in Column K = $5,000 - $1,400 = $3,600 - Comm. This 3-day transaction yielded a % return on cost = 3,600/1,400 = 214%.

US Bond Future Options WWI-Triggered Debit Spread

A segment of the US Bond Futures spreadsheet is used in which a Call Debit Spread is triggered by the WWI < 20 on one day when the spread was opened by Buying 1 C104 and Selling 1 C105 for a computed Cost = N * $/Pt * PremDel = 1 * 100,000 * 80/64= $125,000, where N = number of options, $/Pt = dollars per point for US Bond Futures, and PremDel = the difference between the Long Premium and the Short Premium. The next day the WWI jumped to 71.20 so the position was closed by selling the 1 Long C104 and buying the 4 Short C105 at close the next day. The Premium Difference at Close = 94/64, making the new value of the Debit Spread = 1 * 100,000 * 594/64 = $146,875. So the Profit computed in Column K = $146,875 - $125,000 = $21,875 - Comm. This 1-day transaction yielded a %return on cost = 21,875/12,5000 = 17.5%.

The margin required to make this trade is $3,000; *nevertheless, I believe you should have at least $100,000 in your account before trading either US Bonds or 10-Year Note future options.*

10-Year Note Future Options WWI-Triggered Debit Spread Position

A segment of the US 10-Year Treasury Note Futures spreadsheet is used in which a Put Debit Spread is triggered by the WWI > 80 when the spread was opened by Buying 1 P111 and Selling 1 P110 for a computed Cost = N * $/Pt * PremDel = 1 * 100,000 * 31/64= $48,438, where N = number of options, $/Pt = dollars per point for US 10-Year Note Futures, and PremDel = the difference between the Long Premium and the Short Premium. Two days later the WWI dropped to 71.20 so the position was closed by selling the 1 Long P111 and buying the 1 Short P110 at close the next-day. The Premium Difference at Close = 32/64, making the new value of the Debit Spread = 1 * 100,000 * 32/64 = $50,000. So the Profit computed in Column K = $50,000 - $48,438 = $1563 - Comm. This 2-day transaction yielded a % return on cost = 1,563/48,438 = 3.2%.

YEN FUTURE OPTIONS WWI-TRIGGERED DEBIT SPREAD POSITION

A segment of the Yen Futures spreadsheet is used in which a Put Debit Spread is triggered by the WWI > 80 when the spread was opened by Buying 10 P935 and Selling 10 P930 for a computed Cost = N * $/Pt * PremDel = 10 * 1,250 * 0.18= $2,250, where N = number of options, $/Pt = dollars per point for Yen Futures and PremDel = the difference between the Long Premium and the Short Premium. The next day the WWI dropped to 70.04 so the position was closed by selling the 10 Long P935 and buying the 10 Short P930 at close the next day. The Premium Difference at Close = 0.25, making the new value of the Debit Spread = 10 * 12,500 * 0.25 = $3,125. So the Profit computed in Column K = $3,125 - $2,250 = $875 - Comm. This 2-day transaction is yielded a % return on cost = 875/2250 = 38.9%.

We presented 10 Examples of WWI-triggered Future Options Debit Spreads with all showing a profit. A longer term study was done of the WWI-triggered Debit Spread strategy for the 10 Future Options. A summary of this study is presented below. The software package SelfAdapFutOp was used for this study. This is an Excel-based software program available from the author at email address: jonsch1@verizon.net

Trading Results for 10 Future Options –WWI-Triggered

* KWHEAT Debit Spread Future Profits = $11,191 for a total of 25 trades, or an average trade = $448 Profit
* CORN Debit Spread Future Profits = $13,024 for a total of 28 trades, or an average trade = $465 Profit
* SOYBEANS Debit Spread Future Profits = $15,667 for a total of 23 trades, or an average trade = $681 Profit
* COFFEE Debit Spread Future Profits = $21,484 for a total of 25 trades, or an average trade = $859 Profit
* GOLD Debit Spread Future Profits = $11,128 for a total of 21 trades, or an average trade = $530 Profit
* CRUDE OIL Debit Spread Future Profits = $7,708 for a total of 20 trades, or an average trade = $385 Profit
* SPX Debit Spread Future Profits = $5,192 for a total of 21 trades, or an average trade = $247 Profit
* US BONDS Debit Spread Future Profits = $194,893 for a total of 16 trades, or an average trade = $12,181 Profit
* US 10-YEAR NOTE Debit Spread Future Profits = $157,893 for a total of 18 trades, or an average trade = $8,732 Profit
* Yen Debit Spread Future Profits = $7,626 for a total of 21 trades, or an average trade = $363 Profit

In this evaluation of the Debit Spread strategy, the trade was triggered for the Call Debit Spread when WWI < 20 and for the Put Debit Spread when WWI > 80. The biggest problem in using this strategy is the condition of *hang up* when the WWI remains more than 80 for many days or the condition of *stick down* when the WWI stays below 20 for many days. These conditions are combated by using the tactic of *triads* for most of the future options, which means the triggered position was opened for *three days.* Then the position would be closed with a profit or loss if there was a *hang up or stick down condition.* This triad (three days) tactic was a method for limiting losses if the market was not moving as rapidly as desired in the direction predicted by the WWI. Remember, when the WWI > 80, this means the market is predicting a drop soon; when WWI < 20 the market is predicting a rise promptly. In the case of the US Bond Future Options and the US 10-Year Note Future Options, then a *duad or a two-day limit loss tactic was used* because of the higher amounts of cost involved for these two future options.

2 Sigma Short Credit Spread Computations for Future Options

The 13-month 2 sigma computations are presented in the sections below in which the 2sig Covered Credit Spreads are presented for each of the 10 Future Options. In each case the 2 sigma values are based on the 13-month Standard Deviation Calculation made using that Excel function already discussed. In the Standard Deviation section of my software, I calculate both the 13-month and 9-month 2 sigmas for the Calls and Puts. The free Orion website for Futures and Future Options (www.orionfutures.com) shows the Expiration Months for the underlying Future as well as the Expiration Months available for the Future Options used. I believe that the 2sig Credit Spread is a potentially profitable strategy to augment the WWI-triggered Debit Spread Strategy for Future Options. The covered credit spreads have a Margin computed from the spread width rather than the value of the underlying futures as is the case with Index and Stock Options previously discussed.

The equation for the Short Call strike price is = 10 * ROUND((B247 + L20)/10,0), where B247 contains the Kwheat closing prices, and L20 is the Call 2 sigma of 43.6. ROUND is the Excel round off function. The equation for the Short Put strike price is = 10 * ROUND((B247 - M20)/10,0), where B247 contains the Kwheat closing prices, and M20 is the Kwheat Put 2 sigma of 70.38. The equation for the Call Initial Credit = $L$25 * 50 * (0.35 - 0.1) and the Put Initial Credit = $L$25 * 50 * (0.7 - 0.35), where $L$25 is the cell containing the number of options, 50 is the dollars per point of option, and the numbers in parenthesizes are the net Call and Put short and long premiums. The total initial credit = $460, the net after commission. The margin is $10,000 computed with the equation: = L25 * 50 * 2 * 10, where L25 is the number of options = 10, 50 is the dollars per point of option, 2 is for the Put and Call side and 10 is the width in points between the short and long strike prices. The % Return of Initial Credit to Margin = 4.6%, annualized = 55.2% return.

SURVEY OF 10 FUTURE OPTIONS FOR 2 SIGMA CREDIT SPREAD STRATEGY

A snapshot of the viability of this strategy for the 10 Future Options is given here. In each of the 10 examples below, the position is opened two days before the July Option Month Expiration. Since Future Options do not all expire on the same date, the next expiration date for each Future Option was chosen. In most cases the expiration date was six weeks away. In each case of the 10 examples given below, the Call and Put 2 sigmas are given in the list near the beginning of this chapter which also tabulates the symbols for the 10 Future. In each of the examples below:

* the Call Credit Spread will be written C420/430, where C420 = Short Call at strike price 420 and /430 = Long Call at strike price 430
* the Put Credit Spread will be written P340/330, where P340 = Short Put at strike price 340 and /330 = Long Put at strike price 330

KWHEAT FUTURE 2 SIGMA Covered Spread

The C420/430, Value = 2.0 – 1.3 = 0.7 = 10 * 50 * 0.7 = $350

The P340/330, Value = 1.5 – 0.5 = 1.0 = 10 * 50 * 1.0 = $500

The Total Initial Credit = $850

The margin = 2 * 10 * 50 * 10 = $10,000, where the 2 is for both the Call and Put side of the spread, 10 is the number of options, and 50 is the $/point for the Grains, and 10 is width of spread.

The % Return on Margin = 100 * 850/10,000 = 8.50%

CORN FUTURE 2 SIGMA Covered Spread

The C270/275, Value = 3.3 – 2.6 = 0.7 = 10 * 50 * 0.7 = $350

The P210/180, Value = 0.1 – 0.1 = 0 *Don't Open, No Put side available*

The Total Initial Credit = $350

The margin = 10 * 50 * 5 = $2,500, where 10 is the number of options, and 50 is the $/point for the Grains, and 5 is the spread width.

The % Return on Margin = 100 * 350/2,500 = 7.0%

SOYBEAN FUTURE 2 SIGMA Covered Spread

The C970/980 None Available, C960/980, Value = 0.4 = 10 * 50 * 0.4 = $200

The P710/700 None Available, P720/700 Value = 10 * 50 * 13.6 = $6800 *Unusually high Premium difference*

The Total Initial Credit = $7,000

The margin = 2 * 10 * 50 * 10 = $10,000, where the 2 is for both the Call and Put side of the spread, 10 is the number of options, and 50 is the $/point for the Grains.

The % Return on Margin = 100 * 7.000/110,000 = 70.0%.

COFFEE FUTURE 2 SIGMA Covered Spread

The C77.5/80, Value = 0.36 = 10 * 350 * 0.36 = $1,350

The P62.5/60, Value = .09 = 10 * 350 * 0.09 = $338

The Total Initial Credit = $1,688

The margin = 2 * 10 * 350 * 2.5 = $9,375, where the 2 is for both the Call and Put side of the spread, 10 is the number of options, and 50 is the $/point for the Grains, and 10 is with of spread.

The % Return on Margin = 100 * 1688/9375 = 18.0%

GOLD FUTURE 2 SIGMA Covered Spread

The C430/435, Value = 0.8 = 10 * 100 * 0.8 = $800

The P385/380, Value = 0.6 = 10 * 100 * 0.6 = $600

The Total Initial Credit = $1,400

The margin = 2 * 10 * 100 * 5 = $10,000, where the 2 is for both the Call and Put side of the spread, 10 is the number of options, and 50 is the $/point for the Grains, and 10 is with of spread.

The % Return on Margin = 100 * 1400/10,000 = 14.0%

CRUDE OIL FUTURE 2 SIGMA Covered Spread

The C44.5/45.0, Value = 0.1 = 10 * 1,000 * 0.1 = $1,000

The P36.5/36, Value = 0.08 = 10 * 1,000 * 0.08 = $800

The Total Initial Credit = $1,800

The margin = 2 * 10 * 1,000 * 0.5 = $10,000, where the 2 is for both the Call and Put side of the spread, 10 is the number of options, and 1,000 is the $/point for the Oil Future Options, and 0.5 is width of spread.

The % Return on Margin = 100 * 1,800/10,000 = 18.0%

SPX FUTURE 2 SIGMA Covered Spread

The C1135/1140, Value = 1.2 = 4 * 250 * 1.2 = $1,200

The P1060/1055, Value = 0.7 = 4 * 250 * 0.7 = $700

The Total Initial Credit = $1,900

The margin = 2 * 4 * 250 * 5 = $10,000, where the 2 is for both the Call and

Put side of the spread, 4 is the number of options, and 250 is the $/point for the SPX and 5 is width of spread.

The % Return on Margin = 100 * 1,900/10,000 = 19.0%

US BOND FUTURE 2 SIGMA Covered Spread

The C115/116, Value = 2/64 = 1 * 100,000 * 2/64 = $3,125

The P102/101, Value = 4/64 = 1 * 100,000 * 4/64 = $6,250

The Total Initial Credit = $9,375

The margin = 2 * 1 * 10,100,000 * 1 = $200,000, where the 2 is for both the Call and Put side of the spread, 1 is the number of options, and 100,000 is the $/point for the US BOND and 1 is width of spread.

The % Return on Margin = 9,375/200,000 = 4.69%

US 10-YEAR NOTE 2 SIGMA Covered Spread

The C115/116, Value = 2/64 = 1 * 100,000 * 2/64 = $3,125

The P106/105, Value = 4/64 = 1 * 100,000 * 3/64 = $4,688

The Total Initial Credit = $7,813

The margin = 2 * 1 * 100,000 * 1 = $200,000, where the 2 is for both the Call and Put side of the spread, 1 is the number of options, and 100,000 is the $/point for the US 10-Year Note Futures, and 1 is with of spread.

The % Return on Margin = 7,813/200,000 = 3.91%

Yen 2 SIGMA 2 SIGMA Covered Spread

The C95.0/95.5, Value = 0.07 = 10 * 1,250 * 0.07 = $875

The P62.5/60, Value = .0 = *there is no viable Put side*

The Total Initial Credit = $875

The margin = 10 * 1,250 * 0.5= $6,250, where the Call side of the spread, 10 is the number of options, and 1250 is the $/point for the Yen, and 0.5 is with of spread.

The % Return on Margin = 100 * 875/6,250 = 14.0%

To summarize the 2 sigma covered credit spreads: it is feasible to use the 2sig Credit Covered Spread, but the variability in $/point, spread width, and expiration dates make it more complex than OEX & Stock Options.

Five-Year Capital Growth Model for Future Options

The Capital Growth Model uses the SPX Futures Options Debit Spread as the basis for computing the monthly profit. The model begins with four options the first month and ends with 44 Options the sixtieth month. The first month profit = $572, assuming a Debit Spread Profit of 0.6 points. The number of spreads increases as the capital grows in an exponential fashion. The model has extrapolated capital values based on the simplistic model described. You should enter your actual trade results each month to give you your actual capital growth. From those numbers, the model will extrapolate your predicted capital growth. So the sheet is dual purpose: (1) provide you with a record of your trades and (2) provide you a prediction of your capital growth using your actual initial capital and the # Opt Incr (number of options increased) = 5 in cell B2. Of course, you may enter a number greater than or less than 5 to suit your own trading style

At the end of the sixtieth month for the Capital Growth Model the monthly profit has grown to $6,292 and the capital has grown to $237,784.

We now have two strategies to use for trading the 10 Future Options: (1) WWI-triggered Debit Spreads, (2) 2sig Covered Credit Spreads. You may start with a modest initial capital of $25,000 and make your capital grow significantly year by year.

Summary

This chapter shows how to do the computations needed for profitable Future Options trading. SelfAdaptiveFutOp Software (Excel Workbook) by Jon Schiller is a possible tool for computing the parameters for trading. The equations used are given so you can create your own Excel-based trading software if you prefer. The WWI-triggered Debit Spread is the best strategy to use with Future options. There are usually one or two monthly targets of opportunity uncovered by WWI. Remember: (1) WWI > 80 triggers a Put Debit Spread. (2) WWI < 20 triggers a Call Debit Spread. The typical % return on cost is usually greater than 25% for a few days trade.

The margins required for Future Options trading are given in the beginning of this chapter. These relatively low Margins give you lots of leverage on your risk capital that you use for Future Options trading.

There was a section describing possible Debit trades and Long Positions using all 10 Future Options, including a summary of the results.

Secondly, I showed you the results of my research into the use of 2sig Covered Credit Spreads as a potential profit generator during Option Months for which the Future Options have an expiration. The margin for these Future Option 2sig Covered Credit Spreads is presented for the 10 Future Options covered in this Chapter. These Credit Spreads are open for a complete Option Month (four or five weeks), so I recommend you never open Credit Spreads on more than one of the Future Options at one time. You may have to take corrective action if the Short Call or Short Put is threatened during unusual market rises or falls.

I recommend you do *paper* trading for a month or two using the software, keeping it updated daily and making *paper* trades to get a feel for how the strategies work in practice. Future Options trading is more complex than Stock Options trading because there is a greater variety of types of Futures for which options are available and the trading parameters vary from Future to Future Option type. After you feel confident, then you can switch to real trading. The author is available on email address jonsch1@verizon.net to answer any questions. Please do not ask for trading advice about specific positions, that is beyond the scope of my help!

CHAPTER 7

CURRENCY TRADING WWI-TRIGGERED

I was fortunate to learn Currency trading from an Expert from Madrid when we were teaching a joint course on the principles of Options Trading and Currency Trading, each for six weeks. I presented the new options strategy of this book and my co-instructor taught currency trading. As we were entering our data in the computers we were using for the class, I discovered that the Welles-Wilder Indicator (WWI) was applicable to buying and selling Currencies. The four main currencies applicable for trading are: Euros, Swiss Francs, Yen, and British Pounds Sterling. All trades are the exchange rate of the foreign currency per dollar. In other words, it's how much of the foreign currency that can be purchased for one dollar. My co-instructor, Francisco, was so enthusiastic about the applicability of using WWI that he added my strategy to his own Excel computer program and charts. I was so encouraged that I added the strategy to this book and to my new software packages that are now available. The WWI trigger as applied to currencies is as follows:

Seven Currency Trading Rules

1. Sell a Lot of Currency when WWI < 20, and buy back in a few days when a profit is realized.
2. Buy a Lot of Currency when WWI > 80, and sell in a few days when a profit is earned.
3. Close the Short Lot of Currency when the WWI rises above 20 within three days after selling the Lot; else go to rule (5).
4. Close the Long Lot of Currency when the WWI drops below 80 within three days; else go to rule six

5. Rule for buying back: when WWI *sticks down below 20* for more than three days, buy back the Lot and take a small loss.
6. Rule for selling: when WWI *hangs above 80* for more than three days, sell the Lot and take a small loss.
7. Always wait at least two trading days before opening a New Currency position after closing an existing Currency position

I have applied the seven trading rules trading using the daily currency values that Francisco provided me from his Excel file and the daily data I have collected from the daily closes of My Yahoo. I have kept the daily currency closing prices updated in my new options software, SelfAdapCur. I have discovered the strategy makes good profits with high returns on Margin. The minimum Margin required to buy one Lot of currency is $1,000 and there are a number of good low commission website brokers. The website Francisco recommended was **mgforex.com**, which permits one month of free paper trading so you can become accustomed to their webpage and try out the strategy for currency trading presented in this chapter. I have found some other good website currency trading brokers including **www.saxobank.com**. Another is listed in the Appendix.

How Much Does a Lot of Currency Cost?

A Lot is the minimum amount of currency that can be bought or sold. The margin (amount required in your website account) is $1,000 for each Lot. Following are the values of the Lots for each of the four currencies:

1. 1 Lot **Euro (EUR)** = 100,000 of the currency. The value in US dollars = 100,000/exchange rate. So if Euro = .8041, then one Lot = 100,000/ 0.8041 = $124,363. The margin = $1,000 so the value to Margin ratio is 124 to one. A high leverage for your trading capital.
2. 1 Lot **Swiss Franc (CHF)** = 125,000. If CHF = 1.2265, then the value in dollars of one Lot = 125,000/1.2265 = $101,916. The margin = $1,000, so the value to Margin ratio is 102 to one.
3. 1 Lot **Japanese Yen (JPY)** = 15,000,000. If JPY = 108.77, then the value in dollars of one Lot = 15,000,000/108.77 = $137,905. The margin = $1,000, so the value to Margin ratio is 138 to one.
4. 1 Lot of **British Pounds (GBP)** = 75,000. So if GBP = 0.5342, then one Lot = 75000/0.5342 = $140,398. The margin = $1,000 so the value to Margin ratio is 140 to one.

APPLYING THESE RULES TO THE EURO

for 22 Months, the following results were obtained for 1 Lot trades:

* Total Profit = $16,000
* Total Trades = 38
* Average Profit per Trade = $421/trade
%Profit/Margin = 100 * 421/1000 = 42.1%
* Average Profit per Month = $727/month
* Number of Gains = 27 Number of Losses = 38 –27 = 11
%Winning Trades = 71.1%

Note: If you cannot accept losses during these hangs above 80 or sticks down below 20 for three days, you should not use this trading strategy.

Euro (EUR) Trading Example 1

* Eur = 0.8116/$, WWI = 17.71 Trigger to Sell 1 lot, Credit = 1 * 100,000/.8113 = $123,113
* Two days later the WWI jumped to 75.60 a strong signal to buy back the lot to close.
* Cost to buy back with Eur = 0.8281 for a Cost = 1 * 100,000/0.8281 = $120,758
* Profit = Credit – Cost = $123,113 - $120,758 = $2,455

APPLYING THESE RULES TO CHF

for 22 Months, the following results were obtained for 1 Lot trades:

* Total Profit = $12,992
* Total Trades = 33
* Average Profit per Trade = $394/trade
  %Profit/Margin = 100 * 394/1,000 = 39.4%
* Average Profit per Month = $591/month
* Number of Gains = 24 Number of Losses = 33–24 = 9
  %Winning Trades = 72.7%

SWISS FRANC (CHF) Trading Example 1

* CHF = 123.64/$, WWI = 18.83 Trigger to Sell 1 lot,
  Credit = 1 * 125,000/123.64 = $101,100
* Two days later the WWI jumped to 63.31 a strong signal to buy back the lot to close.
* Cost to buy back with CHF = 125.34 for a Cost = 1 * 125,000/125.34 = $99,729
* Profit = Credit – Cost = $101,100 - $99,729 = $1,371

Applying These Rules to Yen (JPY)

for 22 Months, the following results were obtained for 1 Lot trades:

* Total Profit = $11,943
* Total Trades = 38
* Average Profit per Trade = $314/trade
  %Profit/Margin = 100 * 394/1,000 = 39.4%
* Average Profit per Month = $553/month
* Number of Gains = 27 Number of Losses = 38–27 = 11
  % Winning Trades = 71.1%

Yen (JPY) Trading Example 1

* JPY = 107.21/$, WWI = 12.16 Trigger to Sell 1 lot,
  Credit = 1 * 15,000,000/107.21 = $139,912
* Two days later the WWI jumped to 43.51 a strong signal to buy back the lot to close.
* Cost to buy back with JPY = 108.09 for a Cost = 1 * 125,000/108.09 = $138,773
* Profit = Credit – Cost = $139,912 - $138,773 = $1,139

APPLYING THESE RULES TO BRITISH POUND (UKP)

for 22 Months, the following results were obtained for 1 Lot trades:

* Total Profit = $7,796
* Total Trades = 29
* Average Profit per Trade = $269/trade
  %Profit/Margin = 100 * 269/1,000 = 26.9%
* Average Profit per Month = $35/month
* Number of Gains = 17 Number of Losses = 29–17 = 12,
  %Winning Trades = 58.6%

BRITISH POUND (UKP) Trading Example 1

* UKP = 0.5690/$, WWI = 81.43 Trigger to Buy 1 lot,
  Credit = 1 * 75,000/0.5690 = $175,747
* The next day the WWI dropped to 50.31 a strong signal to sell the lot to close.
* Credit to sell with UKP = 0.5627 = 1 * 75,000/0.5627 = $177,175
* Profit = Credit – Cost = $177,175 - $175,147, = $1,968

As Francisco and I were teaching a short course, we also discovered that Currency **Hedges** work using the WWI as a trigger. The best Currency Hedge is the Euro minus Yen Hedge. One Hedge = Selling 1 Lot of Euro and Buying one Lot of Yen. So one Euro-Yen Hedge cost = 100,000/Euro – 15,000,000/Yen which is a net cost. When Euro = .8518/$ and Yen = 109.05/$, then the net cost = $20,153.

The seven rules for trading Yen-Euro Hedges are similar to those for the trading the four currencies and are given below:

1. Buy a Hedge when WWI < 20, and buy back in a few days when a profit is realized. To buy the Hedge You *buy 1 Lot of Yen and sell 1 Lot of Euro. This is a Long Hedge*
2. Sell the Hedge when WWI > 80, sell in a-day or two when a profit results. To sell the Hedge You *sell 1 Lot of Yen and buy 1 Lot of Euro. This is a Short Hedge.*
3. Close the Long Hedge when the WWI rises above 20 within three days after selling the Lot; else go to rule five.
4. Close the Short Hedge when the WWI drops below 80 within three days; else go to rule six
5. Rule for Closing Long Hedge: when WWI *sticks down below 20* for more than three days, *close Long Hedge by selling 1 Lot of Yen and buying 1 lot of Euro, and take a small loss..*
6. Rule for Closing Short Hedge: when WWI *hangs above 80 for more than three days close the Short Hedge by buying 1 Lot of Yen and selling 1 Lot of Euro, and take a small loss*
7. Always wait at least two trading days before opening a New Hedge position after closing an existing Hedge position

The margin for 1 Lot of hedges is $2,000, which is $1,000 for the Yen Lot and $1,000 for the Euro Lot.

APPLYING THESE RULES TO THE YEN-EURO HEDGE

for 22 Months, the following results were obtained for 1 Lot Yen, 1 Lot Euro Hedge trades:

* Total Profit = $13,486
* Total Trades = 36
* Average Profit per Trade = $375/trade
  %Profit/Margin = 100 * 375/2,000 = 18.75%
* Average Profit per Month = $613/month
* Number of Gains = 26 Number of Losses = 36–26 = 10,
  %Winning Trades = 72.2%

Yen-Euro HEDGE Trading Example 1

* HEDGE WWI = 80.85 Trigger to Sell 1 lot Hedge, Credit = $16,228
* Two days later the WWI dropped to 41.39 a strong signal to close the Short Hedge by buying back.
* Cost to Close the Hedge = $14,311
* Profit = Credit – Cost = $16,228 - $14,311, = $1,917

Please note the Credit and Costs for the Hedge positions are much less than for the Currency Lot positions, because the hedge consists of buying one currency lot and selling another currency lot.

My SelfAdaptCur Software has a sheet for each of the following currencies relative to the US dollar:

1. Euro/$ A Lot of Euro = 100,000
2. Swiss Franc/$ A Lot of SFranc = 125,000
3. Yen/$ A Lot of Yen = 15,000,000
4. UK Lb/$ A Lot of UK Lb = 75,000
5. Yen-Euro Hedge/$ Buy a Lot of Yen and Sell a Lot of Euro for one Hedge Position

In addition to these five sheets, two special sheets called CapitalGrowth and CapGrwthChart are provided to aid you in extrapolating your expected profits three years into the future. The Capital Growth sheet can be used for keeping track of your actual profit and losses to show your actual Capital in dollars. This sheet uses a simplistic model based on the Currency WWI-triggered position. The extrapolation assumes you begin with $4,000 initial capital and 1 Lot of Currency for the WWI-triggered Buys or Sells. The algorithms will adjust the number of Lots based on your initial capital, and the capital growth computations will be adjusted also. The numbers of Lots are increased one each quarter of the year. You may adjust this increase in number of Lots for more aggressive trading or decrease the number of lots for more conservative trading. The Capital Growth Model results are presented below. It assumes that the Euro per dollar is traded and each time the capital in your trading account increases by $4,000, then you increase the number of Lots by one. It is assumed you start with $4,000 in your account, even though only $1,000 Margin is required for 1 Lot Currency trades.

An abbreviated version of this Spreadsheet is presented in the table below.

Time	**Capital**	**#Lots**	**Profit/Mo.**	**Margin**
1st Mo.	$4,000	1	$900	$1,000
1st Year	$26,402	3	$2,676	$3,000
2nd Year	$68,501	5	$4,345	$5,000
3rd Year	$130,063	7	$5,907	$7,000

As may be seen, the Capital grows from the initial $4,000 in the account trading at the level of 1 Lot to a Capital of $130,063 in the three years the model is extrapolating the trading results for Euros. This model shows the huge leverage that can be obtained on your capital: a growth by a factor of 32.51 in three years or a factor of 10.84 per year.

The Capital Growth sheet has extrapolated capital values based on the simplistic model described above. You should enter the actual trades results each month to give you your actual capital growth. The model will extrapolate your predicted capital growth. So the sheet is dual purpose: (1) to provide you with a record of your trades and (2) to provide you a prediction of your capital growth using your actual initial capital and the number of Lot Increases, for which you may enter a number greater than one to suit your own trading style.

THE CURRENT MARKET DATA SHEET

After the Capital Growth Chart (CapGrwthChart) is a sheet in the Self-Adaptive Currency (SelfAdapCur) workbook called Current Market Data (CurrentMktData) for entering the current day's market for the four currencies (the Euro, SFranc, Yen, & UKLB) and the Yen-Euro Hedge. You may use these sheets for entering the realtime end-of-day market data from the Yahoo website my.yahoo.com, or from some other market data web page. My middle son taught me you can customize your my.yahoo.com website to include those currencies, stocks or indices you wish.

You may copy the closing value of the currencies into the row of today's date in Column B which contains the market data, then click on *PASTE SPECIAL, VALUE* in that cell B. The cells are the same in all currency spreadsheets, which makes using the software easier for the user. The daily update takes only a few minutes per day.

COMMON FORMAT FOR THE 5 EXCEL SPREADSHEETS

Columns: A B C D E F G H I J K L M N

Column A has the date in the format: 30 Aug 04

Column B has the underlying market name, for example: Euro, SFranc, Yen, UKLB.

Column C computes **up** the market movement using the equation: = IF((B7 - B6) > 0,B7 - B6,0)

Column D computes the **down** market movement using the equation: = IF((B7 - B6) < 0,B7 - B6,0)

Column E computes the **Up 7-day exponential moving average** using the equation: = E6 * 0.75 + C7 * 0.25

Column F computes the **Down 7-day exponential moving average** using the equation: = F6 * 0.75 + D7 * 0.25

Column G computes the **Welles-Wilder Indicator (WWI)** using the equation: = 100 * (E7/(E7 - F7))

Column H contains the number of Currency Lots set to 1; the value of the Lot in currency/dollar is in cell H1. For the Euro H1 = 100,000/$, for SFranc H1= 125,000/$, for Yen H1 = 15,000,000/$, and for UKLB H1= 75,000/$

Column I computes if the WWI < 20 using the equation: = IF($G7 < 20,5 * ROUND($B7/5,0),"")

Column J computes if the WWI > 80 using the equation: = IF($G7 > 80,5 * ROUND($B7/5,0),"")

Column K computes the triggered Currency trade using the equation: = H239 * $H$1/B239

Column L computes the profit for the trade using the equation: = K246 - K239, where K246 contains the value of selling 1 Lot of the currency to close the Lot previously bought and K239 is the value of buying 1 Lot of currency when in this example WWI had triggered a Buy (WWI < 20) 7 trading days earlier.

Column M computes the cumulative profit for the trades to the present.

Column N computes the average profit/month. For the Euro, the average profit per month was $1,672 for 11 months.

Notes:

1. The row numbers (6 and 7 in the above formulas) depend on the row number of the date for the day of the computation.
2. The values depend on the underlying market value in Column B, Row 7 for the date of 18 Oct 02 for the above spreadsheet example.
3. The dates in the spreadsheets begin with 17 Oct 02 which is row 6, the first date for which there is data for the OEX and the 9 stocks.
4. In order to simplify the date algorithm, holidays are included if they fall on Monday through Friday and the market value in Column B is set equal to the previous market value.

STANDARD DEVIATION COMPUTATIONS FOR CURRENCY

The 2 Standard Deviation (2 sigma) Computation which is a measure of the currency volatility is given in the special segment of each of the 4 currency spreadsheets. The Columns used are O, P and Q. The Standard Deviation (sig) is computed using Excel's STDEV function using the last 10 months. For the Euro, the Up 2 sig = 0.0310 and the Down 2 sig = 0.0344

How to Use the Common Format Spreadsheets

Each day you should enter the closing market values of the Euro, SFranc, Yen, and UKLB for today's date on their respective spreadsheets. The sheets have a unique feature that extrapolates the future market value for each sheet for its respective currency. This extrapolation is based on the previous 20 days using the following equation: = SUM(B232:B251)/20, where B232:B251 are the market values over those 20 days and SUM is the Excel function for summing values over a range of cells; by dividing this sum by 20 it computes the average value for the last 20 days to provide the estimated value. I find this a handy guide to tell me where the market is headed during the remainder of the Option Month, since each market chart shows the value of the underlying currency to the next options expiration date (the expiration dates are used so that if you are doing both currency and options trading you have a common date base to use.

EURO CHART WITH WWI & 20-DAY MOVING AVERAGE

An example of the Euro Chart is presented below.

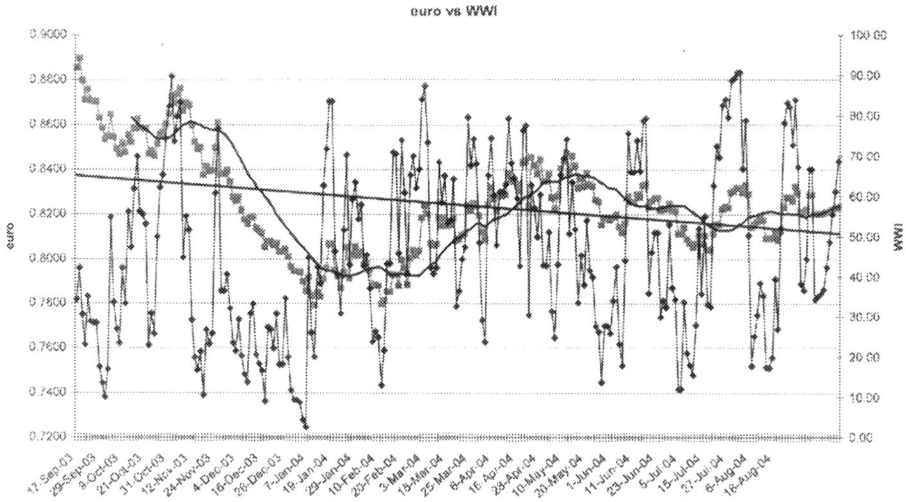

The smooth curve is the 20-day moving average for the currency and is superimposed on the currency line during the extrapolated portion of the currency; the other curve is WWI.

For those who request the Currency Charts, I will email these charts as an attachment for a small handling charge. These charts include:

* Swiss Franc Chart with WWI & 20-day Moving Average
* Yen Chart with WWI & 20-day Moving Average
* British Pound (Lb) Chart with WWI & 20-day Moving Average
* Yen-Euro Hedge Chart with WWI & 20-day Moving Average

The Yen-Euro chart shows the Hedge on the left y-axis with the 20 DMA trend line, the WWI on y-axis 2 for the dates 18 Jul 03 through 16 Oct 03. The Hedge uses a 20-day extrapolation algorithm for both the Euro and the Yen to plot the Hedge curve after the last day of entered data.

The Hedge spreadsheet Columns A through P compute the information for Hedge trading:

Col A = Date

Col B = Euro Value

Col C = Cost of 1 Lot of Euro = $B$4 * $C$3/B461, where B4 = 100,000, C3 = # Lots = 1, B461 contains current Euro Value

Col D = Yen Value

Col E = Cost of 1 Lot of Yen = $D$4 * $C$3/D461, where D4= 15,000,000, C3 = # Lots = 1,

D461 contains current Euro Value

Col F = value or Hedge = E461 - C461, where E461 is current cost of 1 Lot of Yen and C461 is the current cost of 1 Lot of Euro

Columns G through H are the Columns for computing the WWI which is computed in Col H with the equation: 100 * I461/(I461 - J461), where I461 is the Up 7-day moving average and J461 is the Down 7-day moving average for the current day.

Col L has the equation: = IF(K461 < 20,F461,""""), signaling when to Buy a Hedge

Col M has the equation: = IF(K461 > 80,F461,""""), signaling when to Sell a Hedge

Col N has the equation: = F461 which computes the value of one hedge in Dollars.

Col M computes the Profit of having opened and closed a Hedge Position as signaled by WWI

Targets of Opportunity: WWI > 80 or WWI < 20

You should scan your four currency spreadsheets and hedge spread daily seeking the WWI triggers which are indicated in the Columns for WWI < 20 and WWI > 80 triggering a potential profitable currency Lot or Hedge position. If you decide to Buy one (or more) Lot, the Buy order should be given to your internet broker. I have found several website currency brokers, but can't recommend one at this time. You may consider opening a trial account which allows one month of free paper trading. Most currency brokers have no commission, but obtain 2 pips for each trade. A pip is the minimum size of the currency. Two pips are given below for the four currencies:

Euro 2 pips = 0.0002 Euros
SF 2 pips = 0.0002 SF
UK Lb 2 pips = 0.0002 UK Lb
Yen 2 pips = 0.02 Yen

SUMMARY

A possible companion to this chapter is the SelfAdaptiveCur Software (Excel Workbook) by Jon Schiller which provides you with an excellent method for generating good profits. Please find below the average profit per month for the paper trades included in the software for the four currencies and Yen-Euro Hedge at the trading level of 1 Lot:

Euro	Swiss Franc	Yen	UK Pound	Yen-Euro Hedge
$727	$591	$314	$35	$613

As may be seen by the table above, the Euro Hedge had the best monthly average profit at $727/mo and the Yen-Euro Hedge had the second best at $613/mo.

The WWI-triggered Buying and Selling has the potential of high profits for low Margin. Remember: (1) WWI < 20 triggers a Sell one or more Lots. (2) WWI > 80 triggers a Buy one or more Lots. After a Buy or Sell, the position should be closed when it shows a profit, which typically takes two or three trading days. The required Margin for one Lot is $1,000; however, I recommend a minimum account size of $4,000 to trade one Lot. Note: for the Hedge trading when WWI < 20, then Buy the hedge and then, after a profit occurs, close the hedge. When the WWI > 80, sell the hedge and when a profit is generated, close the position. I recommend a minimum account of $4,000 to trade one Lot of Yen-Euro Hedge.

I recommend you do *paper* trading for a month or two using the software, keeping it updated daily and making the *paper* trades, thus getting a feel for how the WWI buy and sell works in practice. After you feel confident, then you can switch to real trading. One website broker, mgforex.com, is a web broker that allows a month of free paper trading when you sign up for their services.

The author is available at email address jonsch1@verizon.net to answer any questions about currency trading or the functioning of the software, SelfAdapCur. Please do not ask for trading advice, that is beyond the scope of my help!

CHAPTER 8

STOCK TRADING USING WWI AS A SIGNAL

As I was writing this book, it occurred to me that the WWI was a signal that could be used for buying and selling stocks as well as currencies. So I did research by paper trading the NASDAQ stocks in the list for one year to see what profits could be obtained by using the WWI as I did for the currencies described in Chapter 7, for the OEX in Chapter 4, and the Stock Options in Chapter 5. The nine of the same stocks of the 13 stocks covered in Chapter 5 were used in this chapter. As I performed this research, I observed the hazard of WWI *hang-up*, where the WWI remains above 80 for more than three days. This *hang-up* can cause a loss. The opposite hazard of *push-down* also occurs when the WWI stays below 20 for more than three days, which can also causes a loss.

This strategy requires finding a low-cost online broker for buying and selling stocks at a low commission. Ameritrade is a potential broker, since they advertise equity (stock) trades for $10.99/trade no matter how many shares. Short-term stock trades require a low commission to be feasible. Also it is necessary to sell the stock shares short when the WWI > 80, so you must have a broker that will permit your account to sell short.

As a result of my research in this strategy, 12 months paper trading, I devised the following four rules that should be followed:

1. When WWI > 80, Sell 200 Shares Short, Buy Back Short Shares when WWI drops below 80 to make a profit within three days.
2. When WWI < 20, Buy 200 Shares, Sell Shares when WWI rises above 20 to make a profit within three days.

3. When WWI > 80 for three days, Close Short Stock Position, take a loss
4. When WWI < 20 for three days, Sell Stock Position, take a loss

The following is a list of the nine NASDAQ stocks used in this paper trading: Amgen, Cisco, Dell, eBay, IBM, Intel, Microsoft, QQQQ, and Oracle. IBM, included in Chapter 5, has the highest price of the nine stocks, over $90/share, and Oracle has the lowest share price, about $12/share in Oct 03.

RESULTS OF APPLYING THIS STRATEGY FOR A YEAR OCT 02

STOCK	#TRADES	YR'S PRFT	PRFT/MO	200 SH CST	ANN %RET	RATING
eBay	21	$3,475	$290	$10,822	32.1%	A+
Intel	24	$1,894	$158	$5,532	32.2%	A+
Msft	23	$1,884	$155	$5,814	32.06%	A+
QQQ	23	$1,486	$124	$6,626	22.4%	B
Amgen	17	$2,456	$205	$13,030	18.8%	B-
IBM	14	$2,950	$246	$18,278	16.1%	C+
Dell	22	$980	$82	$6816	14.4%	C-
Oracle	17	$198	$17	$2,328	8.51%	D
Cisco	21	- $230	- $19	$4,118	- 0.475	F

The ratings are given for the nine stocks: A+ means an annual return of greater than 30%, B means an annual return greater than 20%, C means an annual return less than 20%, D means an annual return less than 10% and F means an annual loss. The three A+ Stocks to use for this strategy are eBay, Intel, and Microsoft. The annual return of over 32% for the three A+ Stocks is comparable to the A+ Mutual Funds such as CMG Focus which has a return of 37%.

The spreadsheet for each of the stocks for Columns A through G (which compute the WWI for the Stocks) is identical to that of the 13 Stock Options covered in Chapter 5; the Columns H and I contain the equations: = IF($G465 < 20,B465,"") & = IF($G465 > 80,B465,""). These equations provide the WWI trigger indications for Buying and Selling the 200 shares of stock respectively.

The 12-month Chart for the eBay is shown below, with the 50-day moving average (the smooth curve), the WWI signal, and the eBay Line Chart. The 50 DMA is a signal which is used by many of the big Mutual Fund managers to buy or sell a stock: *when the stock curve crosses below the 50 DMA they dump the stock (sell); when the stock curve crosses above the 50 DMA they buy the stock.*

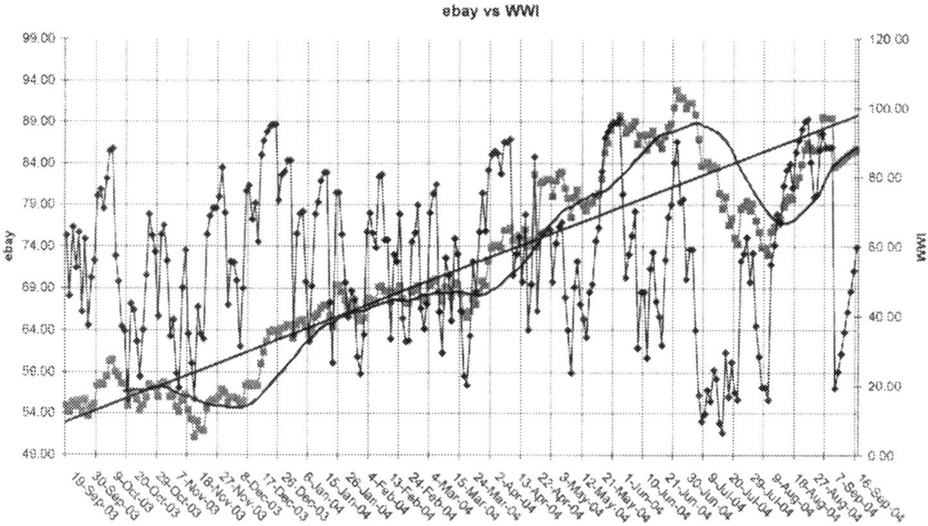
ebay vs WWI
ebay
WWI
99.00
94.00
89.00
84.00
79.00
74.00
69.00
64.00
59.00
54.00
49.00
120.00
100.00
80.00
60.00
40.00
20.00
0.00
19-Sep-03
30-Sep-03
9-Oct-03
20-Oct-03
29-Oct-03
7-Nov-03
18-Nov-03
27-Nov-03
8-Dec-03
17-Dec-03
26-Dec-03
6-Jan-04
15-Jan-04
26-Jan-04
4-Feb-04
13-Feb-04
24-Feb-04
4-Mar-04
15-Mar-04
24-Mar-04
2-Apr-04
13-Apr-04
22-Apr-04
3-May-04
12-May-04
21-May-04
1-Jun-04
10-Jun-04
21-Jun-04
30-Jun-04
9-Jul-04
20-Jul-04
29-Jul-04
9-Aug-04
18-Aug-04
27-Aug-04
7-Sep-04
16-Sep-04

Strategy of Buying & Holding Stocks as Long-Term Equity Investment

I also devised a strategy that did not require so much of my time. I decided to try buying 200 shares of these same nine stocks and to hold on to them. My research showed me this was more profitable. You probably do not want to buy all the stocks on the list, but would prefer to concentrate on one or two of the highest performing ones. The eBay stock, which was the second best profit maker of the nine stocks, is included below as an example:

Initially 200 shares were purchased for $11,630 equity value. eBay had a two-for-one split about seven months later in Oct 2002, so the 200 shares became 400 shares. By the end of June 2004 the eBay stock = 91.95/share, so the 400 shares had an equity value = 400 * 91.95 = $36,780. The profit over that two-year period = $25,150, or a %Return = 216%. Better than any of the Hi Tech Mutual Funds such as CMG Focus. As I said in the Stock Options Trading chapter, when a stock you are holding splits, your value is automatically adjusted so you do not lose because of the split.

Buying and Holding a High-Performance Mutual Fund

The *International Business Daily* has an excellent section on Mutual Fund Performance. **CGM Focus** was first of the ***Top 13 Growth Funds*** in October 2003. I tracked the mutual funds for over a year, and I found CGM Focus to be the highest profit maker in that time with an annual growth rate of 72%. The growth of CGM Focus was A+ in both the last three months and the last 12 months categories. It would be a safe investment, since it has total net assets of 480 million dollars. In October 03 CGM Focus closed at 27.68. It had risen 236% in the last five years or up an average of 54%. You might want to invest in such as this Mutual Fund as a profitable, trouble-free investment. For example, if you bought 200 shares that would cost about $5,500 at 27.5 per share. If the growth continued at the rate of 78% per annum, that fund should be worth $13,065 assuming a 35% ordinary tax rate on dividends and a 20% long-term rate on capital growth.

How Does Buy and Hold Cmg Focus Compare with Top Best Buy and Hold Stocks?

The top two stocks, Intel and eBay, were somewhat better than CGM Focus over the same time period:

* Intel 107.7% Return
* eBay 98% Return
* QQQQ 87% Return
* Cisco 87% Return

So these 4 stocks out-performed the CGM Focus 72% return over the same period of time.

SUMMARY

As shown in this chapter, my research shows that buying and selling the nine stocks, Amgen, Cisco, Dell, eBay, IBM, Intel, Microsoft, QQQQ, and Oracle, when signaled by the WWI was profitable for all the stocks except Cisco which had a small loss.

The research presented in this chapter also shows that for these nine stocks, a more profitable and much simpler strategy is to buy 200 Shares of the stock and hold them for profit, except for Microsoft, which made $338 more trading profit than equity growth. The total equity increase for the buy and hold strategy was almost twice the total WWI trading strategy profits for the nine stocks.

The best two stocks to use for the Buy and Hold strategy were Intel and eBay, with annual growths of 107.4% and 98.3% respectively over the year period of the research. The next two best strategy growth stocks were QQQQ and Cisco with both over 46% annual growth on initial investment cost. All four of these highest growth stocks had A or A+ ratings. The best two performers had a 62% higher annual growth than CMG Focus, the top IBD listed Hi Tech Mutual Fund in October 03. The second best pair had an annual growth rate of 62% .

I believe it is important to use your investment capital for different markets and different strategies. This chapter adds two new procedures for buying and selling Hi Tech Stocks to make your capital grow. Most options brokers permit you to use 70% of the value of the equity stocks as Margin for your other types of options trading.

CHAPTER 9

SURVEY OF MARKET SIGNAL INDICATORS

DESCRIPTION OF EACH MARKET SIGNAL INDICATOR

In this book so far we have emphasized the use of the Welles-Wilder Indicator for deciding when to open Debit Spreads for OEX, Stock or Future Options. The WWI you see in the examples and software in this book used the 7-day WWI, which means the "7-day exponential moving average." There is also the 14-day WWI which means the "14-day exponential moving average" that could be used. In addition there are a number of other market indicators that also can be used to decide when to open positions. A survey of these other signal indicators will be presented in this chapter.

Recently I became very interested in the application of academic neural network theory to financial markets. I combined the above indicators in a multi-input three-layer neural network to make a powerful overall market trend indicator which I will explain later in this chapter.

When I lived in Spain I had options trading software that used all of these other market indicators. Since returning to California, however, my research has convinced me that profitable trading can be accomplished using the 7-day WWI. For those of you who would like to use the other market indicators, I have prepared a software package called SelfAdapSigIndicOEX. I furnish this package free to anyone who orders any one my other new options software packages, if requested.

The OEX (S&P 100) index options are the best trading vehicles because of the large open interest and daily trading volume. Typically the open interest of the Calls and Puts together is over a million options and the daily volume is between 20% and 30% of the open interest or 200 to 300 thousand options. This large trading volume assures good liquidity, allowing you to open new positions or change existing positions easily.

We shall present you the same algorithms for computing trading signals as used by the Program Traders in New York that drive the market daily by dumping in or extracting billions of dollars, causing the market to jump or drop. The program traders are particularly active during the first hour and the last 15 to 20 minutes of the NY market session. The principle market signal indicators used are included in this chapter's survey:

1. The 4-day Moving Average Difference = Mad4
2. The Difference between the 9-day and 4-day Moving Averages = Mad4-9
3. The Moving Average Difference Comparison = MADC, which is a
c omparison between the
4. 20-day and 40-day exponential moving averages.
5. The Stochastics %D minus %K (special moving average indicators) difference
6. The 7-day Welles-Wilder Indicator (WWI), which is a Relative Strength Indicator (RSI), will be covered in this chapter to show it's relevance to the other market signal indicators. The WWI shows when the OEX or other Underlying Market is overbought or oversold.
7. The Bollinger Band Indicator (BBI) is another indicator that tells when the market is overbought or oversold. The BBI chart has an Upper Band and a Lower Band. When the OEX is above the Upper Band, then the market is overbought, when the OEX is below the Lower Band, then the market is oversold. So the Up Band corresponds to the WWI > 80 and the Low Band corresponds to WWI < 20.

The Excel Spreadsheet in the Signal Indicator workbook uses Columns A through AD to compute the 6 market indicators listed above.

* Mad4 uses Columns B, D, and E
* Mad4 - 9 uses Columns E, F, and G
* MADC uses Columns H through L
* Stochastics%K - %D uses Columns M through U
* WWI uses the computations coupled over from my Workbook SelfAdapStkOp, equations described in Chapter 3
* Bollinger Bands use the Columns B and V though AC

MOVING AVERAGE DIFFERENCE MARKET INDICATORS

All four of the Moving Average Difference market indicators (the first four in the above list) make use of the exponential moving average of different numbers of days. The algorithms for the more complex indicators will be given below.

The four-day moving average difference (Mad4), the 9-day - 4-day MAD (Mad4 - 9), the MADC, and Stochastics %K - %D are indicators which change sign to tell when the market is in an up trend or down trend. When the market indicator switches from negative to positive, this is called a *golden cross* and is the signal that the market is moving up. The golden cross corresponds to the WWI < 20. When the indicator switches from positive to negative, this is called the *death cross* and is the signal that the market is moving down. The death cross corresponds to the WWI > 80.

THE 4-DAY MOVING AVERAGE DIFFERENCE = MAD4

The simplest moving average difference market indicator, which is also used to indicate when to open a Call Debit Spread or Put Debit Spread (or Long Call or Long Put), is the MAD4. This is the difference between the OEX and the 4-day exponential moving average. The algorithms for this moving average difference indicator are given in Chapter 3. Each chart also shows the 20-day moving average curve. The equations for the MAD4 indicator are:

= B464 - D464, where B464= OEX, D464 = 4 Da Exponential MA = B464 * $D$3 + D463 * $D$2, where D2 and D3 are the 4-day MA constants, D463 is the-day before 4 Da MA.

Difference Between the 9-day and 4-day Moving Averages = MAD9-4

This market signal indicator uses the difference between the 9-day exponential moving average and the 4-day exponential moving average. The equations for the MAD4 indicator are:

= D464 - F464, where D464 = 4 Da Exp MA, and F464 = 9 Da Exp MA

The Moving Average Difference Comparison = Madc

This indicator uses the difference between the 20-day exponential moving average and the 40-day exponential moving average, then takes the 13-day exponential moving average of that difference. The final parameter or MADC is the difference between the Ma20-40 and its 13-day moving average. It is a longer term indicator than the Mad4 and MAD9-4. The equations for the MADC are given below:

= $H$3 * B465 + H464 * $H$2, which computes the 10-day exp MA

= B465 * $I$3 + I464 * $I$2, which computes the 20-day exp MA

= I465 - H465, which computes the difference between the 10-day and 20-day exp MAs in Col J

= J465 * $K$3 + $K$2 * K464, which computes the 13-day exp MA in Col K

= J465 - K465 which computes the MADC in Column L

The Chart for the MADC & OEX versus Time is below; the bar chart is the MADC, the irregular curve is OEX and the smooth curve is the 20-day moving average.

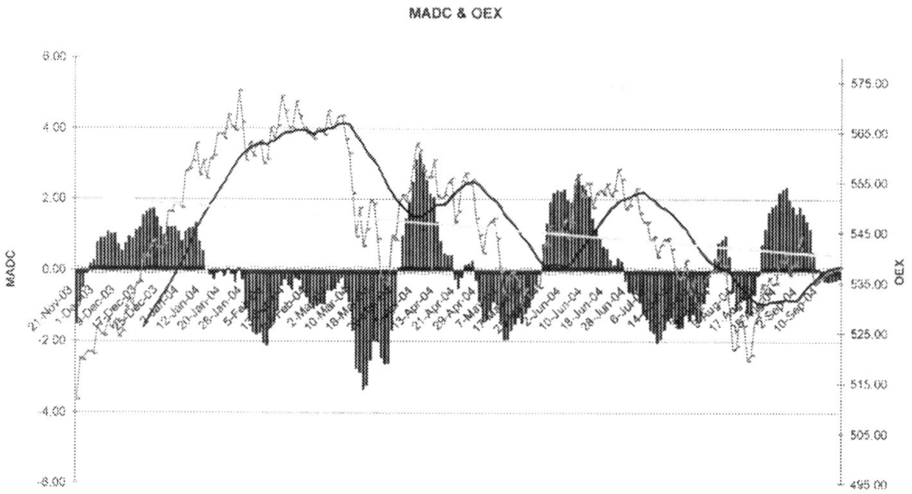
MADC & OEX
MADC
OEX
6.00
4.00
2.00
0.00
-2.00
-4.00
-6.00
575.00
565.00
555.00
545.00
535.00
525.00
515.00
505.00
495.00

The Stochastics %K - %D (Special Moving Average Indicators) Difference

The Stochastics%K - %D is the most complex of the market indicators. The following computations are made in Columns M through U:

* 5-day Maximum, equation: = MAX(B7:B11), where MAX is the Excel Maximum function
* 5-day Minimum, equation: = MIN(B7:B11), where MIN is the Excel Minimum function
* 3-day exponential moving average of the 5-day (Max – Min), equation: = $O$3 * (B11 - N11) + $O$2 * O10, where cells O3 and O2 contain the 3-day exponential moving average functions fl and f2, B11 is the OEX and N11 contains the 5-day Min.
* The equation for the 3-day exponential moving average for the difference between the Max and Min is given by the equation: = $O$3 * (M11 - N11) + P10 * $O$2, where M11 - M11 is the difference, O3 and O2 contain the fl and f2 for the 3-day exponential moving average and P10 is yesterday's 3-day exponential moving average.
* The equation for Column Q is given by the equation: = $O$3 * O11/P11 + Q10 * $O$2, where Columns O and P contain the 3-day exponential moving averages of the difference between OEX and the 5-day Minimum, and the 3-day exponential moving average of the difference between the 5-day Maximum and 5-day Minimum.
* Column R contains the computation for the %K of the Stochastics algorithm with the equation: = 100 * (B11 - N11), where B11 is today's OEX and N11 is today's 5-day Minimum of the OEX.
* Column S contains the computation for the %D of the Stochastics algorithm with the equation: = 100 * O11/P11, where O11 contains the 3-day exponential moving average of the difference between the OEX and the 5-day Minimum of the OEX.
* Column T contains the computation for the 3-day exponential moving average of %K given by the equation: = R11 * $T$3 + T10 * $T$2, where T3 and T2 contain fl and f2 of the 3-day exponential moving average, R11 is today's %K and T is the computed value.
* Finally Column U contains the result: the Stochastics%K - %D computation given by the equation: = R11 - T11, where R contains the %K and T contains the 3-day exponential moving average of %K.

This very complex set of algorithms yields this Market Signal Indicator that tells you whether the market is in an Up trend or Down trend.. The Stochastics is a very sensitive indicator in that it has wide swings from plus to minus for relatively small changes in the market.

BOLLINGER BAND INDICATOR

The Bollinger Band algorithm uses a 39-day exponential moving average of the OEX (or other market), the difference between the OEX and the 39-day moving average, and the 17-day 2 Standard Deviation of the difference.

The Upper Bollinger Band is the sum of the 39-day moving average and the 2 Standard Deviation. The Lower Bollinger Band is the difference between the 39-day moving average and the 2 Standard Deviation. The equations are:

* = V463 + C464, which computes the cumulative difference in the OEX in Col V
* = B464 * $X$3 + W463 * $X$2, which computes the 20-day MA of OEX in Col W
* = B464 - W464, which computes the 20-day MAD of OEX in Col X
* = 2 * STDEV(X447:X464), which computes the 2 sigma for the 20-day MAD over the last 18 days in Col Y
* = W464 + Y464, which computes Up Bollinger Band value in Col Z
* = W464 - Y464, which computes the Down Bollinger Band value in Col AA
* = IF(B464 > Z464,(B464 - Z464),0), computes how much the OEX is overbought in Col AB
* = IF(AA464 > B464,(B464 - AA464),0), computes how much the OEX is oversold in Col AC

The Bollinger Band Chart can be created by charting OEX and the Up Band and Down Band. The Bollinger Band Chart can be compared with the WWI Chart and both show close agreement when indicating the market is overbought or oversold.

WELLES-WILDER INDICATOR (WWI) MARKET INDICATOR

To reiterate the use of the WWI: when the WWI > 80 this is a prediction of an imminent drop in the market and when the WWI < 20 this is a prediction of an imminent rise in the market.

Appendix D gives a comparison of the ability of the Bollinger Band Indicator and the Welles-Wilder Indicator to signal when the market is overbought or oversold. Although there was a lot of correlation between the two indicators, it appears that the WWI is more sensitive in giving the triggers for overbought and oversold.

Neural Networks

I became very interested in the application to academic neural network theory applied to financial markets. As a result of my neural network research, I devised a 5 Input, 3 Layer, 1 Output Feed Forward Neural Network using the following market signal indicators as the first layer of Inputs:

* Mad4, layer 1 weighting = 0.632911
* MAD9-4, layer 1 weighting = 0.387597
* MADC, layer 1 weighting = 2.50000
* Stochastics%K - %D, layer 1 weighting = 0.010635
* WWI, layer 1 weighting uses two logic equations: = IF(B9 > 80,1,0) in Row 9 and = IF(B9 < 20, - 1,0), in Row 10

The weighting in Layer 2 = 1/3 for the first four inputs, the fifth input uses the equation: = SUM(F5:F8) + SUM(C9:C10) which computes the value for cell F11 used in the final output value.

The weighting in Layer 3 = 10

The Final Output weighting = 10, The Final Output Value of the Neural Network = F11 * G5, where F11 was computed above and G5 is the final output weighting.

If the final output is greater than 10, this means an *Up Trend market*. If the final out put is less than –10, this means a *Down Trend market*. If the final output is between –10 and + 10, then *the market is trendless*.

This Network is portrayed using the following logic equations: = IF(H5 < - 10, - 1,0), or = IF(H5 < - 10, - 1,0), which are displayed in cells I5 or J5 for the Down or Up Trend, respectively.

So with the equations in this chapter you may create your own Neural Network to signal a reliable indication of the market trend.

SUMMARY

We have surveyed some additional market signal indicators and compared them with the Welles-Wilder Indicator (WWI). The market signal indicators are:

* Mad4
* Mad4-9
* Madc
* Stochastics%K - %D
* Bollinger Band Indicator
* Welles-Wilder Indicator

I included a unique Neural Network for predicting Market Trends which uses four of the Up and Down signal Indicators and the WWI *overbought oversold indicator* described with equations.

There are a number of other market indicators that my previous software packages computed such as Japanese Candlestick indicators.

Although these other market signal indicators give additional insight into the market behavior, it is possible to make all your trading decisions using the WWI. The principle thrust of this book is that you can make a good profit trading Index Options, Stock Options, Future Options, and Currencies using: (a) the 2 sigma Covered Credit Spread for generating a good monthly income and (b) using Debit Spreads (or currency Lots) triggered by the Welles-Wilder Indicator. All of these other market signal indicators give a graphical picture of the market behavior, but are not necessary for making a good trading profit.

Chapter 10

Some Tips to Enhance Trading Profits

The purpose of this chapter is to share with you some tips I have learned during more than 20 years of Options trading. The two principle strategies are: (1) the use of 2 sigma Credit Spreads for Index Options and Future and Stock Options and (2) the use of WWI-triggered Debit Spreads for Index Options, Future Options and WWI-triggered Long Stock Options and Currency Lots. The monthly income generator is the use of OEX 2 sigma Credit Spreads. The WWI-triggered trades are targets of opportunity to augment the monthly income generated by OEX 2 sigma Credit Spreads.

Use Daily Volatility to Increase Covered Credit Spread Premiums

You should make the daily volatility work for you. *How much does the daily volatility make the OEX swing?* The daily swing is the difference between the Daily High and Daily Low. Typical swings during a 5 week Option Month in July were:

* Monday after Expiration:
  Swing = 538.61 – 533.94 = 4.67, Hi - Cls = 2.32 and Cls - Lo = 2.35
* Tuesday after Expiration:
  Swing = 539.81 – 535.10 = 4.71, Hi - Cls = 0.16 and Cls - Lo = 4.55
* Wednesday after Expiration:
  Swing = 544.04 – 533.02 = 11.02, Hi - Cls = 11.02 and Cls - Lo = 0
* Thursday after Expiration:
  Swing = 536.99 – 529.43 = 7.56, Hi - Cls = 1.5 and Cls - Lo = 6.06

Or an average swing for those 4 sample days = 6.99 points.

In opening a new OEX 2 sigma covered spread near the beginning of a new Option Month we can make that daily swing work for us to obtain a **higher** *initial Call Premium Difference* and *initial Put Premium Difference. How do we do this?* You would take the closing Call Spread Premium difference and Put Spread Premium difference for the day before you want to open your new Call and Put covered credit spreads and add a small increment to each value. The daily swing will help you get that increment on each side. In some cases you may not get both sides filled the same day. For example, if the Call swing was large and the Put swing was small, you might get the Call spread filled, but not the Put side filled. That's okay, there's no reason that both have to be filled the same day. Since expiration is about four or five weeks away, you have plenty of time to get both sides filled using volatility to help you increase the premium received when filled.

An Example of Letting Volatility increase the Premium Difference you obtain in filling your order:

On Monday, the Call Premium Difference = 0.7 and the Put Premium Difference = 0.6. On the next day (Tuesday) before open place the order for the Call Premium Difference be 0.7 + 0.2 = 0.9; the Put order Premium Difference = 0.6 + 0.3 = 0.9

So what happened? On Tuesday, the market started out down, so the Put Premium difference increased and the Put side of the Credit Spread was filled at 0.9, so the Put Initial Credit was 0.9 * 10 * 100 = $900, for 10 options, which was = 0.3 * 1,000 = *$300 more than you would have received if you hadn't used the market volatility to fill at a higher Premium Difference.* Later that same day, the market turned around and went up, so then the Call Credit Spread was also filled at 0.9 = 0.9 * 1,000 = $900, which was 0.2 = $200 more than without using the upward market volatility. This example shows how we used volatility to make $500 more in the beginning of the options month than you would have received just asking for the premiums existing at the beginning if the day. *This is a tactic that makes your broker work for you.*

When to Open the Triggered Debit Spread

The fact that the Chicago Options Exchange closes 10 minutes after the NY Stock Exchange Floor closes is a big advantage for opening Debit Spreads. You may enter the NY closing value for the stocks being tracked and the Futures being tracked to discover new WWI triggers as a result of the day's market action. Remember WWI > 80 triggers Put Debit Spreads for OEX or Future Options or ATM Long Puts for Stocks. WWI < 20 triggers Call Debit Spreads for OEX or Future Options or ATM Long Calls for Stocks. You then have time in that last 10 minutes the Options Exchange is open to place your order and you have time to get the order filled before options close.

What Are the Difficulties in Getting Debit Spread Orders Executed in That Last 10 Minutes?

There's a great deal of scrambling to get orders filled during that end-of-day activity. If you read the fine print of these website brokers that promise execution within 9 or 10 seconds, you will find they have lots of excuses for **NOT** meeting their guarantee of quick execution such as "high volume at end of day."

The Premium differences between the Long Position and the Short Position are sometimes quite different when you compare the closing value difference with the Bid and Ask value difference. The later may be 0.1 or 0.2 less than the former. So that means what you *thought* should be a fair difference isn't executed because it was more than could be actually fulfilled. One way of always getting the Debit Spread order filled is to place a *market order*. This means your broker can fill the order at whatever premium comes up. I personally never use market orders, since I feel there are too many chances of not being treated fairly. A sample *market order* is given below:

Buy 10 October eBay Puts at 55 and Sell 10 October eBay Puts at 52.5 (the next lowest strike price) *at market*. This Debit Spread order will always be filled at whatever market difference exists between the P55 and P52.5 at the time the order is entered by the broker. For example, you may be disappointed since you had expected the market difference to be 1.15, but the market order was filled at 1.35. For 10 options you had expected to pay $1,150 + Commission when actually you paid $1,350 + Commission. So by placing a market order, you take whatever is given. I don't recommend market orders because you give up control over what you will pay. *Many brokers charge less commission for market orders than for* ***limit orders*** *because they don't have to work as hard to fill the order.*

When you place a limit order or an order to fill at a specified premium difference, you always get the specified premium difference or a more favorable difference. In other words, you may get better, but never worse, when placing a limit order.

When to Close an Open Debit Spread (or Long Position)?

It is always best to close a Debit Spread or Long Position as soon as you make a good profit. A good rule of thumb is given below:

1. If you opened a Put Debit Spread or a Long Put when WWI > 80, then if WWI drops below 60 in a few days, then close and take your profit.
2. If you opened a Call Debit Spread or a Long Call when WWI < 20, then if WWI rises above 40 in a few days, then close and take your profit

Normally you would make a short-term profit by closing in a few days about half the maximum possible from the Debit Spread. In other words, if you had an OEX Debit Spread 5 points wide, (example Long Call 520 and Short Call 525 for which you paid 2.5 points) the maximum profit you could make = 5 - 2.5 = 2.5 Points. So if you opened 10 Debit Spreads for 2.5 points, then the cost = $2,500 + Comm. If you held the position until expiration and the OEX finished above 525, then your profit = (5 - 2.5) * 10 * 100 = $2,500 – in-out commission. However, if the OEX had finished below 520, then the Debit Spread would have finished worthless and you would have lost the initial $2,500 + Comm paid for the position. Debit Spreads are a short-term (a few days) strategy. *Take your profit and run!* Typically the short-term profit for a 5 point OEX Debit Spread would be 1.1 point, so for 10 OEX Debit Spreads, the profit = 1.1 * 10 * 100 = $1,100 – in-out Comm = $1,100 - $140 = $960.

Remember, when WWI > 80 open a Put Debit Spread, and when WWI < 20 open a Call Debit Spread. So when triggered, open the Debit Spread. When a profit is made in a few days close the position to lock in the profit.

Sounds easy, doesn't it? What is the Hazard?

The hazard for Put Debit Spreads is the *hang-up* condition, when the WWI rises above 80 and stays high for three or more days. This means the underlying market is overbought for three or more days and the option premiums are decaying, which reduces the possibility of making a profit. I recommend closing out the Put Debit Spread if the WWI is *hung-up* above 80 for three days, take a loss and try again later. I call this the **triad** strategy: hold a hung-up Put Debit Spread only three days, close with loss.

There is a similar hazard for the Call Debit Spread. The *stuck-down* condition is when the underlying market remains at a WWI < 20 for more than three days. Premium decay will cause a loss. So the strategy is to close the Call Debit Spread and take your loss – the same *triad* strategy.

This three-day close out of hung-up or stuck-down conditions will limit your losses of Debit Spreads opened. The WWI > 80 predicts the market is going to drop, but sometimes it takes too long to make a profit from the triggered Put Debit Spread. The same is true when the WWI < 20 predicts the market is going to rise.

Corrective Action for 2 Sigma Covered Credit Spreads

The 2 sigma Covered Credit Spread is our regular monthly income producer. If the underlying 100 stocks of the S&P 100 (OEX) Index were a random process, then the probability of the OEX closing higher than the 2 sig Short Call or lower than the 2 sig Short Put would be about 5%. In other words each 20 months the Short Call or Short Put would be threatened with a finish in-the-money (ITM) of either the Call or Put side.

Unfortunately the threats to the Call or Put side occur more often than every 20 months. Why do you experience these threats? There are two reasons:

1. The stock market isn't a purely random process; it is driven by unusual events such as the September 11 terrorist attack or the 1987 panic sell-off of the market. Or more normally unusual Profit Reports by key companies or losing financial reports can cause extraordinary jumps or drops in the market. These occurrences cause the market to rise or fall more than 2 sigma during the Option Month.
2. Sometimes you *cheat* a little and make the Short Call or Short Put closer than 2 sigma, because as an experienced options trader you see that you can make more initial credit if you make the short 5 or 10 points closer to the market than the 2 sigma computation would indicate. You shouldn't do it, but it's human nature to try to extract a little more profit.

What Do We Do When a Short Put or Short Call Is Threatened?

The first intelligent action is to check the WWI value of the underlying market. If the Call is threatened and the WWI > 80 then the market will self correct and drop below the current level. So no action will be necessary since the WWI predicts a drop will take place.

Similarly if the Put is threatened and the WWI < 20, no action will be necessary since the WWI predicts a rise will take place.

If you are only a day or two from expiration, you may want to take corrective action when a Call or Put is threatened as a conservative action.

One *hazard* of the OEX moving so that the Short Put or Short Call of the Covered Credit Spread is ITM is the *Early Assignment* which your broker automatically executes closing the Short Put or Call with no warning to you. I have learned about this hazard the hard way when my broker performed the early-assignment execution on a stock covered credit spread which was executed in *cash to buy the stocks*, so I had to sell the stock and pay commission for the selling. Fortunately for OEX covered credit spreads, the early assignment is executed in cash, so you do nothing except suffer the loss caused by the automatic execution.

Corrective Action for Credit Spreads If WWI Is Between the Limits of 80 and 20

When the market is neither overbought nor oversold, you should take corrective action when the Credit Spread is threatened; in other words, the market is above the Short Call or below the Short Put. If the Call is threatened during the 10 minutes after the New York market closes and while the Chicago Options market is still open, you should close out the threatened Call Credit Spread and Open a new higher strike price Credit Spread. To accomplish this you buy back the old Short Call and sell the old Long Call, then sell a new Call at Strike Price 5 or 10 points higher than the old Short Call and buy a new Call cover at the next strike price above the new Short Call.

If the Put is threatened during the 10 minutes after NY closes and the Chicago Options market is still open, you should close out the threatened Put Credit Spread and Open a new lower strike price Credit Spread. To accomplish this you buy back the old Short Put and sell the old Long Put, then sell a new Put at Strike Price 5 or 10 points lower than the old Short Put and buy a new Put cover at the next strike price below the new Short Put. Unfortunately, this type of corrective action almost always results in a loss for the Option Month.

What Would Be the Cost of a Weak Corrective Action?

Take an example using OEX closing with the Short Call 1.89 points in - the - money (ITM). The Short C500, Long C505 position is threatened because the closing OEX = 501.89. The C500/C505 = (10.2 - 8.3) – 2.2 points, which would be the cost to close the old C500/C505 credit spread. Or for 10 options the cost = 2.2 * 10 * 100 + Comm = $2,200 + 70 = $2,270. The new Covered Credit Spread of Short C505, Long C510 has a premium difference = (8.7 - 6.8) = 1.9. So the net cost of the corrective action = 1.9 – 2.2 = – 0.3 points or for 10 options, the **net cost** would = .3 * 10 * 100 = $300 + Comm = $440. If we assume the original Initial Credit = $700, then the Net Initial Credit has been reduced to $700 - $440 = $260. Not a loss, but the potential profit was reduced by over a factor of two by the corrective action

What Would Be the Cost of a Strong Corrective Action?

A strong corrective action is needed when the penetration of the Short Call or Put is > 2 points. In this case close out the threatened Call as before, but now open the New Call Covered Credit Spread 10 points higher. In this example, let's assume the same Call Credit Spread of C500/C505, but now the market closes at 503.92 or a penetration of the Short C500 of 3.92 points. Close the old C500/C505 and open a new Credit Spread C510/C515 (Short C510 and Long C515). The Close out of the Old C500/C505 costs 3.3 points or for 10 Options, the Close out Cost = 3.3 * 10 * 100 + 70 = $3,370. The new credit for the New C510/C515 = 2.1 points, or for 10 Options, the Initial Credit = $2,100 - $70 Comm = $2,030. So the **net cost** of the Corrective Action = 2,030 - 3,370 = - $1,340. If the Initial Credit had been = $700, now the **net loss** for the Option Month = 1,340 - 700 = $640.

The above two examples show how to take corrective action when threatened. A similar corrective action would be taken if the Put side of the 2 sigma Covered Credit Spread were threatened. Let's look at a weak and strong corrective action for a Short Put 475 Long Put 470. Let's say the OEX closed at 473.99, a weak penetration of 1.01 points, with the P475/P470 premium difference = 3.2 or a **cost to close** for 10 Options = 3.2 * 10 * 100 = $3200 + $70Comm = $3,270. To open the new P470/P465 = 2.2 points or for 10 Options a New Initial Credit = $2,200 - 70Comm = $2,130 So the net Cost of the corrective action = $3,270 - $2,130 = $1,140. If the initial Credit of the original Credit Spread had been $700, now the **net loss** would be $440.

Summary

1. Check to see if the WWI signals the market is overbought or oversold. If WWI < 20 and the Put is threatened by a penetration, then no corrective action is necessary, unless the expiration is only one or two days away. If WWI > 80 and the Call is threatened by a penetration, then no corrective action is necessary, unless the expiration is only one or two days away. If expiration day is imminent, take corrective action.
2. For a weak threat, penetration less than 2, move the Call Spread one strike price higher or the Put Spread one strike price lower.
3. For a strong threat, penetration greater than 2, move the Call Spread two strike prices higher or the Put Spread two strike prices lower.
4. Out-of- the-Money (OTM) options are all premium with no inherent value which decay to zero at options expiration Friday (third Friday of the month). This decay to zero is what you want for Covered Credit Spreads, since if the Premiums end worthless, then the amount you received when the credit spreads were opened becomes your profit.
5. For WWI-triggered Debit Spreads or Long Calls or Puts, the premium decay is irrelevant since the positions are only kept open for a few days until profit is realized during which time premium decay is small.
6. The hazard of Debit Spreads is the hung-up or stuck-down condition of the WWI which prevents a profit. When this happens you should always close a Debit Spread after three days to limit the loss. In such a condition, you will experience a small loss, but a larger loss which would result from premium decay is avoided.
7. The Hazard for ITM Short Calls or Short Puts is *Early Assignment* in which your Short Calls or Short Puts are bought back automatically by your broker without getting permission from you.

Chapter 11

Global Growth Model

Using the three markets covered in this book, we have examined two strategies that make your capital grow rapidly. You may want to specialize in one of the markets or you may want to broaden your trading and cover all three markets. I personally plan to spread my trading and cover Index and Stock Options, Future Options, and Currencies. I also plan to buy 200 shares of one of the high performing Tech Stocks and watch the investment capital grow. You should consider these three markets a place to use **Risk Capital** with the help of the strategies covered in this book. These three markets and two strategies are an excellent way to obtain leverage of your risk capital.

The three Capital Growth Models summarized in this chapter should be considered as *goals* for your trading. You should strive to meet the goals, but not be disappointed if you don't achieve them. You should also plan to use the Capital Growth models as **record keepers** for your actual trading results. Options and Currency trading is always more difficult than it appears to be when you study the strategies. But believe me, I've been option trading for almost 25 years now, and it does become easier with the passage of time as you gain experience in the vagaries of the market. One of the most important lessons to learn is how to accept the inevitable occasional trading losses. I've tried to explain methods to limit the losses when an adverse market threatens your trading positions. Be sure you *use* the loss-limiting tactics. Don't just sit and hope. If a position is threatened, *take action to limit the loss.*

In this chapter we will examine the three capital growth models, in which it is assumed you begin with $25,000 Initial Capital in each of the market areas:

1. Growth Model for Index Options (OEX) and the nine Stock Options: Amgen, Cisco, Dell, eBay, IBM, Intel, Microsoft, QQQQ, and Oracle. My software has added Yahoo to the list.
2. Growth Model for Future Options of the Underlying Futures: KC Wheat, Corn, Soybean, Coffee, Gold, Lt. Sweet Crude Oil, Gold, SPX, US Bonds, US 10 Yr. Notes, and Yen.
3. Growth Model for Currencies: Euro, Swiss Franc, Yen, British Pound, and the Yen-Euro Hedge.

Finally, in the last section of this chapter, the Global Growth Model, it is assumed you allocate your capital between the three market areas as follows: $25,000 to Index and Stock Options, $25,000 to Future Options, and $4,000 to Currency trading or a total of $54,000 Initial Capital. The period of time for the Growth Models is from October 04 through September 08 or a total of four years.

OEX and Stock Options 4-year Growth Model

This growth model assumes that you trade OEX 2sig Covered Credit Spreads with the Short Call 2sig above the market and the Short Put 2sig below the market at the beginning of the options month; the Call Cover or Long Call is 5 points higher than the Short Call and the Put Cover or Long Put is 5 points lower than the Short Put. Furthermore, it is assumed the total Call plus Put Premium difference is 1.0 or an average of 0.5 points for the Call side and 0.5 points for the Put side. It is assumed the Initial Credit received when the position is opened results in a Profit at expiration.

A second assumption is that only one Long Call or Long Put triggered by the WWI is used to generate an additional monthly profit added to the monthly profit of the OEX Covered Credit Spread. It is assumed the level of profit obtained by the short-term Long Call or Put is 0.5 points. It is assumed the Commission level is $70 for one side of a Covered Spread and is adjusted proportionally as the number of Options increases as the capital grows. A similar commission level is assumed for the Longs.

Using the OEX and Stock Options 4-Year Growth Model, the Initial $25,000 increases to $221,382. This is a an average annual growth rate of 221.38%.

Commodity Future Options Growth Models

This growth model assumes that only one Call Debit Spread or Put Debit Spread is triggered by the WWI each months from one of the other Future Options. For purposes of the model, it is assumed that SPX Future Options are used to generate an additional monthly profit added to the monthly profit of the SPX Future Option Covered Credit Spread. It is assumed the level of profit obtained by the short-term Debit Spread is 0.6 points. It is assumed the commission level is $70 for one side of a Covered Spread and is adjusted proportionally as the number of Options increase as the capital grows. A similar commission level is assumed for the Debit Spreads.

Using the Commodity Future Options Growth Model, the initial $25,000 account Capital grows to $237,784 after four years or an average annual growth of 187%.

Currency Growth Models

The currency growth model assumes that you begin trading **One Lot** of currency which requires a Margin of $1,000, but that you begin with $4,000 capital in your account to avoid the danger of Margin calls should the market go against an initial buy or sell. Furthermore it is assumed the Euro is used and the beginning trade change in Euro is .00900 so that for one Lot trade profit = $900 which is given by the equation = O4 * $O$2 * N4, where O4 is the trade change of .00900, $O$2 is = 100,000, the number of Euros per Lot of Currency, and N4 is the number of Lots in the trade.

A second assumption is that only one profitable Currency trade is made per month. Also it is assumed that each time the capital increases by $4,000, then the number of Lots increase by one. For the model the number of beginning Lots is 1 and of ending Lots is 9. The initial Margin is $1,000 and the final Margin is $9,000 or one thousand dollars per Lot.

Using the Currency Capital Growth Model that the Initial Capital is $4,000 and that after four years the capital has grown to $208,133 which is an average annual capital growth rate of 1300%. This growth model has the highest annual growth rate of any of the trading markets.

GLOBAL CAPITAL GROWTH MODEL

As explained above, the Global Growth Model assumes the initial capital is $54,000 which is allocated as follows: $25,000 for OEX and Stocks Options, $25,000 for Future Options, and $4,000 for Currency trading. Using the Global Capital Growth Model, the Initial $54,000 grows to $1,074,367 after four years. An average annual growth of $268,562 and an average annual growth rate of 497%.

Summary

The Options and Currency trading strategies covered in this book give you an opportunity to take $54,000 of **risk capital** and make it grow to more than **one million dollars**. The three individual growth models used conservative parameters, but none assumed a monthly loss, which is probably not completely realistic. Nevertheless, with careful trading discipline, you should see a healthy growth in your risk capital.

CHAPTER 12

SELF-ADAPTIVE TRADING SOFTWARE

Three packages available from author as email attachments as excel files:

* SelfAdapStkOp, SelAdaptFutOp, SelfAdapCur with user manuals
* 2 Bonus Packages with any of above Packages
* SelfAdapStockTrading, SelfAdapSigIndicOEX with user manuals

These software packages will be discussed in turn below.

Self-Adaptive Index & Stock Options Software: SelfAdapStkOp

This software is available as email attachment. Each file is about 1.5 MB or less. It requires Windows + Excel programs on your computer. The software is for the S&P 100 (OEX) index options and for 10 Hi Tech common stock options. This software uses two basic strategies:

1. Two Sigma Covered Credit Spreads for Generating Monthly Income
2. Debit Spreads or Long Options triggered by the Welles-Wilder Indicator (WWI) for short-term profit (a few days).

Each sheet of the software has the computations for the 2 sigma, the computations for the WWI and an indication of whether a Put or Call Debit Spread is triggered by the WWI being greater than 80 or less than 20..

A quick review of the strategies:

Two Sigma Call Covered Credit Spread: Sell the Call options at the strike price 2 sigma above the market and buy the same number of Call options the next strike price higher than the Short Call strike price. This position results in an Initial Credit. If the market expires below the Short Call, the Initial Credit received when the position is opened becomes profit. Normally used for OEX options, this strategy can also be used for Tech stock options.

Two Sigma Put Covered Credit Spread: Sell the Put options at the strike price 2 sigma below the market and buy the same number of Put options the next strike price lower than the Short Put strike price. This position results in an Initial Credit. If the market expires above Short Put the, Initial Credit received when the position is opened becomes profit. Normally used for OEX options, this strategy can also be used for Tech stock options. Since the 10 stocks chosen are growth stocks, a possible modification to the strategy is to use only Put Credit Spreads closer to the market than 2 sigma. *This is riskier than using Short Puts 2 sigma below the market at time of opening the position.*

Call Debit Spread triggered when WWI < 20: Buy Call Options at-the-money and sell Call options at the next strike price above for a net debit. If the market rises as the WWI predicts it will, then a profit will result when the position is closed, unless option premium decay causes a loss. Normally used for OEX options.

Put Debit Spread triggered when WWI > 80: Buy Put Options at-the-money and sell Put options at the next strike price below for a net debit. If the market drops as the WWI predicts it will, then a profit will result when the position is closed, unless option premium decay causes a loss. Normally used for OEX options.

Long Call triggered when WWI < 20: Buy Call Options at-the-money for a net debit. If the market rises as the WWI predicts it will, then a profit will result when the position is closed, unless option premium decay causes a loss. Normally used for one of the 10 Common Stock Options.

Long Put triggered when WWI > 80: Buy Put Options at-the-money for a net debit. If the market drops as the WWI predicts it will, then a profit will result when the position is closed, unless option premium decay causes a loss. Normally used for one of the 10 Common Stock Options.

This Software has 14 Sheets for calculating trading parameters and a Chart for each of the following Options:

1. OEX (S&P 100) Index Options
2. Amgen Stock Options
3. Cisco Stock Options
4. Dell Stock Options
5. DNA Stock Options
6. eBay Stock Options
7. Intel Stock Options
8. IBM Stock Options
9. Microsoft (Msft) Stock Options
10. Nasd100Tr (QQQQ) Stock Options
11. NetFlix Stock Options
12. Oracle Stock Options
13. SINA Stock Options
14. Yahoo Stock Options

In addition to these 14 sheets and 14 Charts, a Special Sheet Called CapitalGrowth and CapGrwthChart is provided to aid you in extrapolating your expected profits through Jan 09 or some five years into the future. The Capital Growth sheet can be used for keeping track of your actual profit and losses to show your actual capital in dollars. This sheet uses a simplistic model based on the OEX and eBay Credit Spreads and the 10 Common Stock Option WWI-triggered Debit Spread or Long Positions. The extrapolation assumes you begin with $25,000 initial capital and 15 options for the OEX Covered Credit Spreads and 10 options for the eBay Covered Credit Spreads and Stock Option Debit Spreads or Longs. The algorithms will adjust the number of options based on your initial capital, which you enter your actual beginning Capital into cell K2 of the CapitalGrowth sheet, and the capital growth computations will be adjusted accordingly. You could begin with less capital, but I recommend you begin with at least $25,000 (and you will get better attention from your broker with that starting amount). The number of options are increased by 5 July and January of each year. You may adjust this increase number for more aggressive trading or less for more conservative trading.

I have recently added a sheet to keep track of multiple Credit Spreads when you open positions for the OEX and several Stock Options such as I did in the Feb 04 Option Month. It computes all the parameters and keeps track of the running profit or loss. I found it was helpful to keep track of intraday or end-of-day profit positions.

After the CapGrwthChart is a sheet called CurrentMktData for entering the current day's market data for the OEX and the 10 stocks. You may use this sheet for entering the realtime end-of-day market data from the Internet using Interquote, or some other market data web page. You may link the value into the row of today's date in Column B which contains the market data by copying the market value and then *PASTE SPECIAL, VALUE* in the cell B248 for the data for 22 Sep 03. The cells are the same in all OEX and 10 Stock spreadsheets, which makes using the software easier for the user.

Common Format for the 11 Excel Spreadsheets

A B C D E F G H I J K L M N

Column B has the underlying market name, for example Amgen, Cisco, Dell, eBay, etc.

Column C computes the market movement up using the equation: = IF((B7 - B6) > 0,B7 - B6,0)

Column D computes the market movement down using the equation: = IF((B7 - B6) < 0,B7 - B6,0)

Column E computes the Up 7-day exponential moving average using the equation: = E6 * 0.75 + C7 * 0.25

Column F computes the Down 7-day exponential moving average using the equation: = F6 * 0.75 + D7 * 0.25

Column G computes the Welles-Wilder Indicator using the equation: = 100 * (E7/(E7 - F7))

Column H computes if the WWI < 20 using the equation: = IF($G7 < 20,5 * ROUND($B7/5,0),"")

Column I computes if the WWI > 80 using the equation: = IF($G7 > 80,5 * ROUND($B7/5,0),"")

Notes:

1. The row numbers 6 & 7 depend on the row number of the date for the day of the computation
2. The values depend on the underlying market value in Column B, Row 7 for the date of 18 Oct 02 for the above spreadsheet example.
3. The dates in the spreadsheets begin with 17 Oct 02 which is row 6, the first date for which there is data for the OEX and the 9 stocks.
4. In order to simplify the date algorithm, holidays are included if they fall on Monday through Friday and the market value in Column B is set equal to the previous market value.

The 2 Standard Deviation (2 sig) Computation and 2 sig Covered Credit Spread Computations are given in the special segment of each of the sheets in columns L, M, and N. Column J is used to compute the cost of the triggered position and Column K is used to compute the profit of the position closed.

The Standard Deviation (sig) is computed using Excel's STDEV function using the last 10 months. In the spreadsheet segment above which goes from cell L1 to N25 the 2 sig Short Call and Short Put strike prices are computed using the following equations:

Short Call: = 5 * ROUND((B247 + L20)/5,0), where B247 contains the OEX value at Option expiration date 19 - Sep - 03 and L20 contains the value of the Call 2 sigma computed with the equation: = 2 * STDEV(L3:L12), where L3 to L12 contains the Maximum variation of OEX for the10 Option months.

Long Call: = L22 + 5, where L22 contains the strike price of the Short Call and 5 is the next higher Call strike price. Note: for stocks that have strike prices closer spaced than 5 points, the 5 would be adjusted accordingly, for example 2.5 for eBay stock.

Short Put: = 5 * ROUND((B247 - M20)/5,0), where B247 contains the OEX value at Option expiration date 19 - Sep - 03 and L20 contains the value of the Put 2 sigma computed with the equation: = 2 * STDEV(M3:M12), where M3 to M12 contains the Minimum variation of OEX for the 10 Option Months.

Long Put: = M22 - 5, where M22 contains the strike price of the Short Put and 5 is the next lower Put strike price. Note: for stocks that have strike prices closer spaced than 5 points, the 5 would be adjusted accordingly, for example 2.5 for eBay.

Note: the same information and equations are included in the spreadsheets for the 10 stocks (Amgen, Cisco, etc.).

The Columns H and I in the spreadsheets are for signaling when WWI has triggered a potentially profitable Debit Spread or Long position. The Column J can be used for computing the cost of opening the Debit Spread or Long position and Column K can be used for computing the short-term profit (or loss) of these short-term positions which are normally open for a few trading days.

The Capital Growth Sheet in the software shows a period from Oct 03 to Oct 08 or a period of five years. Assuming no losses and the number of options increased each six months as five, this model shows with a beginning capital of $25,000 at the end of five years your capital would have grown to $322,960. As mentioned in the introduction, you may use this spreadsheet to keep track of your actual profits and losses to a chart of your actual profit growth and number of options traded.

The CapitalGrowth sheet has extrapolated capital values based on the model described above. You should enter the actual trades results each month to give you your actual capital growth. The model will extrapolate your predicted capital growth. So the sheet has dual purpose: (1) provide you with a record of your trades and (2) provide you a prediction of your capital growth using your actual initial capital and the # Opt Incr= 5 in cell B2 which you may enter a number greater than or less than 5 to suit your own trading style.

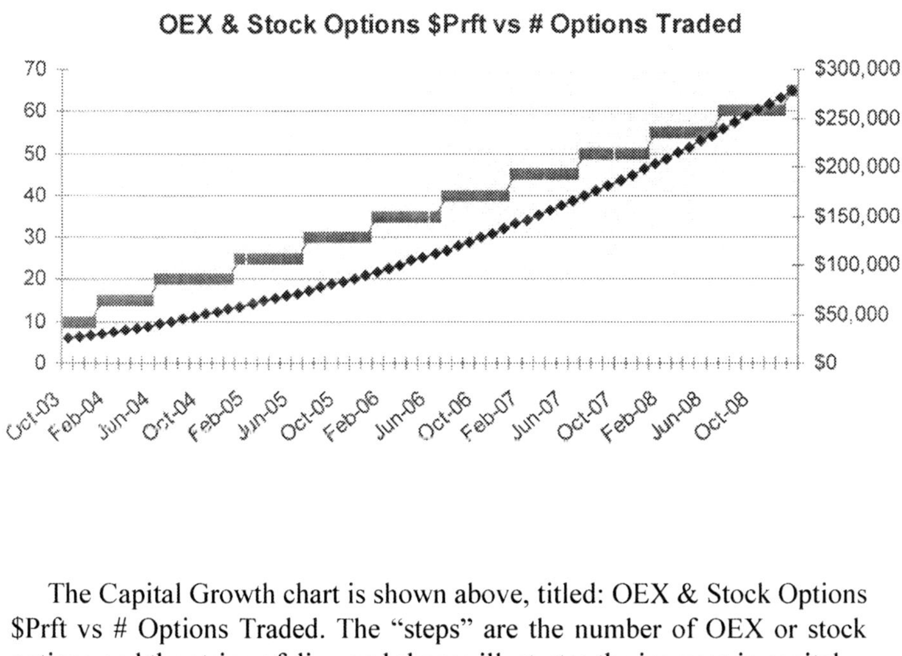

The Capital Growth chart is shown above, titled: OEX & Stock Options $Prft vs # Options Traded. The "steps" are the number of OEX or stock options and the string of diamond shapes illustrates the increase in capital.

HOW TO USE THE COMMON FORMAT SPREADSHEETS

The common format was shown above. Each day you should enter the closing market values of the OEX, Amgen, Cisco, Dell, eBay, IBM, Intel, Msft, QQQQ, Oracle and Yahoo on the line for today's date.

The sheets have a unique feature that extrapolates the future market value for each sheet for its respective stock (or OEX). This extrapolation is based on the previous 20 days using the following equation: = SUM(B232:B251)/20, where B232:B251 are the market values over those 20 days and SUM is the Excel function for summing values over a range of cells; by dividing this sum by 20 it computes the average value for the last 20 days to provide the estimated value. I find this a handy guide to tell me where the market is headed during the remainder of the Option Month, since each market chart shows the value of the underlying stock or OEX to the next expiration date.

At the beginning of the options month, you should open a 2 sigma OEX Covered Credit Spread, the strategy described on the first page of this chapter. Your objective is to open a Call credit spread and a Put credit spread obtaining the greatest initial credit possible. It is *not* necessary to open both the Call and Put sides of the credit spread at the same time or even on the same day. Here is a tip to increase your monthly profit: check the 2 sig OEX Call and Put Short Strike Prices and the Long Call Strike Prices, and check your market data website for the new month's premiums for the four strike prices and insert these values in the Call and Put equations that calculate the Initial Credit that would be received. Rather than use these premiums for the order you place with your website broker, increase the value by 0.1 pr 0.2 more than is quoted. This way the daily volatility and the increased volatility at the beginning of a new Option Month will help you obtain more initial credit and therefore more profit at the expiration of the new Option Month. **The margin** for 15 OEX 2 sig covered credit spreads = 5 * 15 * 100 * 2 = **$15,000.** I recommend you have double the margin amount in your account to open a credit spread.

You may want to open Covered Credit Spreads for one of the Stocks as well. eBay appears to be the best stock to use for credit spreads because of it's wide spread of strike prices to allow a 2 sig covered credit spread and the strike prices are 2.5 points apart meaning that for 10 options **the margin** for both the Call and Put side = 2.5 * 10 * 100 * 2 = **$5,000**. So using my rule of double the margin in your account, to open both the OEX and the eBay credit spreads you would have a **total Margin = $20,000** or an amount = **$40,000** in your account.

Targets of Opportunity: WWI > 80 or WWI < 20

You should scan your 11 market spreadsheets daily seeking the WWI triggers which are indicated in the Columns H for WWI < 20 triggering a potential profitable Call Debit Spread or Long Call. If you decide to open such a position, the Long Call would be at-the-money, or the Call strike prices closest to the market.

An example: in scanning the sheets on Th 18 Sep 03, the day before Sep options expiration, the Dell sheet showed a WWI = 80.94 and cell I246 showed a value 35 indicating a Long Put 35 for Dell would be a potentially profitable position to open. A position was opened by buying 10 Dell Oct Put 35 for a cost = $1050, computed by the equation: = 10 * 1.05 * 100, where 10 is the number of options, 1.05 is the premium of P35, and 100 is the $/point for stock options. Oct options were used because the nearness of the Sep expiration would have made Sep options unsuitable because of the rapid decay in premiums values at the end of the Sep Option Month. Two trading days later on Mon 22 Sep 03 the WWI = 40.46 signaling that the market had dropped as predicted and the Long Put 35 should be closed by placing an order to sell the 10 Oct Dell P35 at the quoted premium = 2.15 meaning the value of the Long Put 35 = $2050 including the round-trip commission cost of $70. This two-trading-day transaction yielded a profit = $1,030 or a return on investment = 98.10%. *This example is typical and shows the potential power of the WWI-triggered long positions for stocks.*

WWI-triggered positions can also be used for OEX, but since ATM Long positions are expensive, it is better to use Debit Spreads, where, for a Put Debit Spread using 10 options, you would buy 10 Puts at the money and sell 10 Puts at a strike price 5 points lower (the next lowest strike price). So WWI triggers allow you to add to your monthly profit.

Summary of SelfAdapStkOp Software

The SelfAdaptiveStkOp Software (Excel Workbook) by Jon Schiller provides you with an excellent method for generating a steady monthly income using the **2 sigma OEX Covered Credit Spread** strategy and augmenting the monthly income with targets of opportunity using the WWI-triggered Debit Spreads or Long positions. Remember: (1) WWI > 80 triggers a Put Debit Spread or Long Put position. (2) WWI < 20 triggers a Call Debit Spread or Long Call position. This software has an OpCmdCntr sheet which keeps track of WWI targets of opportunity and covered credit sheets on a single easy to view sheet.

FUTURE OPTIONS SOFTWARE: SELADAPTFUTOP.XLS

This software is available as email attachment. Each file is about 1.5 MB or less. It requires Windows + Excel programs on your computer. The software is for 10 Commodity Future Options. This software uses two basic strategies:

1. Two Sigma Covered Credit Spreads for Generating Monthly Income
2. Debit Spreads or Long Options triggered by the Welles-Wilder Indicator (WWI).

Each sheet of the software has the computations for the 2 sigma, the computations for the WWI and an indication of whether a Put or Call Debit Spread is triggered.

Two Sigma Call Covered Credit Spread: Sell the Call options at the strike price 2 sigma above the market and buy the same number of Call options the next strike price higher than the Short Call strike price. This position results in an Initial Credit. If the market expires below the Short Call, the Initial Credit received when the position is opened becomes profit. You must use only those Commodity Futures that have expiration dates during the current month. Many of the Futures have expirations bi-monthly or quarterly.

Two Sigma Put Covered Credit Spread: Sell the Put options at the strike price 2 sigma below the market and buy the same number of Put options the next strike price lower than the Short Put strike price. This position results in an Initial Credit. If the market expires above Short Put the Initial Credit received when the position is opened becomes profit. You must use only those Commodity Futures that have expiration dates during the current month. Many of the Futures have expirations bi-monthly or quarterly.

Call Debit Spread triggered when WWI < 20: Buy Call Options at-the-money and sell Call options at the next strike price above for a net debit. If the market rises as the WWI predicts it will, then a profit will result when the position is closed, unless option premium decay causes a loss. It is okay to use options with expirations more than one month in the future, since this is a short-term strategy in which the position is closed after a few days for a profit (or loss).

Put Debit Spread triggered when WWI > 80: Buy Put Options at-the-money and sell Put options at the next strike price below for a net debit. If the market drops as the WWI predicts it will, then a profit will result when the position is closed, unless option premium decay causes a loss. It is okay to use options with expirations more than one month in the future, since this is a short-term strategy in which the position is closed after a few days for a profit (or loss).

This Software has a Sheet for each of the following Future Options:

1. Kwheat Future Options
2. Corn Future Options
3. Soybeans Future Options
4. Coffee Future Options
5. Gold Future Options
6. Light Sweet Crude Oil Future Options
7. SPX Future Options
8. US BOND Future Options
9. US 10-YEAR NOTE Future Options
10. Yen Future Options

In addition to these 10 sheets, two special sheets called CapitalGrowth and CapGrwthChart are provided to aid you in extrapolating your expected profits five years into the future. The Capital Growth sheet can be used for keeping track of your actual profit and losses to show your actual Capital in dollars. This sheet uses a simplistic model based on the Future Option WWI-triggered Debit Spread. The Extrapolation assumes you begin with $25,000 initial capital and 10 options for the Stock Option Debit Spreads. The algorithms will adjust the number of options based on your initial capital, and the capital growth computations will be adjusted. The number of options are increased by 5 July and January of each year. You may adjust this increase number for less or more aggressive changes.

After the CapGrwthChart is a sheet called CurrentMktData for entering the current day's market data for the 10 Futures whose Options are used. You may use this sheet for entering the realtime end-of-day market data from the Internet using a web page containing the Commodity Future Prices. You may link the value into the row in Column B which contains the market data by copying the market value and then *paste special value* in the cell B248 (for sample date 22 Sep 03). The cells are the same in all 10 Future spreadsheets, which makes using the software easier for the user.

COMMON FORMAT FOR THE 11 EXCEL SPREADSHEETS

A B C D E F G H I J K L M

Column A has the date for each trading day

Column B has the underlying market name, for example Amgen, Cisco, Dell, eBay, etc.

Column C computes the market movement up using the equation: = IF((B7 - B6) > 0,B7 - B6,0)

Column D computes the market movement down using the equation: = IF((B7 - B6) < 0,B7 - B6,0)

Column E computes the Up 7-day exponential moving average using the equation: = E6 * 0.75 + C7 * 0.25

Column F computes the Down 7-day exponential moving average using the equation: = F6 * 0.75 + D7 * 0.25

Column G computes the Welles-Wilder Indicator using the equation: = 100 * (E7/(E7 - F7))

Column H computes if the WWI < 20 using the equation: = IF($G7 < 20,5 * ROUND($B7/5,0),””")

Column I computes if the WWI > 80 using the equation: = IF($G7 > 80,5 * ROUND($B7/5,0),””")

Notes:

1. The row numbers 6 and 7 depend on the row number of the date for the day of the computation
2. The values depend on the underlying market value in Column B, Row 7 for the date of 18 Oct 02 for the above spreadsheet example.
3. The dates in the spreadsheets begin with 17 Oct 02 which is row 6, the first date for which there is data for the 10 Commodities.
4. In order to simplify the date algorithm, holidays are included if they fall on Mon through Fri and the market value in Column B is set equal to the previous market value.

The 2 Standard Deviation (2 sig) Computation and 2 sig Covered Credit Spread Computations are given in the special segment of each of the sheets in columns L, M, and N. Column J is used to compute the cost of the triggered position and Column K is used to compute the profit of the position closed

The Standard Deviation (sig) is computed using Excel's STDEV function using the last 10 months. In the spreadsheet segment above which goes from cell K1 to N25 the 2 sig Short Call and Short Put strike prices are computed using the following equations:

Short Call = 5 * ROUND((B247 + L20)/5,0), where B247 contains the Future value at Option expiration date 19 - Sep - 03 and L20 contains the value of the Call 2 sigma computed with the equation: =2 * STDEV(L3:L12), where L3 to L12 contains the Maximum variation of the Future for the option 10 months.

Long Call = L22 + 5, where L22 contains the strike price of the Short Call and 5 is the next higher Call strike price. *Note:* for Future options that have strike prices closer spaced than 5 points, the 5 would be adjusted accordingly: for example, 1 is the spacing for 10 Year Notes and the Corn future Options have strike prices 10 apart. Also many of the Future Options don't have monthly expirations, but have bi-monthly or quarterly expirations. One would not use 2 sigma Covered Credit Spreads for Future Options which do not have the current Option Month for expiration. Corn has bi - monthly expirations so Oct and Dec would be good Option Months for Corn credit spreads. Also the dollars per point and number(#) of Options traded are given in cells D1 and F1 which are different for the different Future Options. For example D1 = 50 for the three grains (KWheat, Corn, and Soybeans) and D1 = 100,000 for the two US Treasury Futures (Bonds & 10Y Notes). Most of the Future Options use F1 = 10, but SPX uses 4, and the two Treasury Futures use F1= 1. The equations used in the computations for the Debit Spreads use the D1 and F1 for the particular Future Options. For example, for LSC Oil the equations for computing the cost of the Debit Spread are: = $F$1 * $D$1 * (0.219), where $F$1 means the cell, where the number of Oil Future Options is contained (#Op = 10). $D$1 is the cell in which the dollars per point for oil are contained ($1,000). Also some of the Future Options have a multiplier between the Future's value and the Future Options value. This multiplier factor is included in the computations for the value of the Long Call or Put strike price. For example the equation for oil is given: = IF($G262 > 80,50 * ROUND(100 * $B262/50,0),""), where the 100 is the multiplier factor for oil.

Short Put = 5 * ROUND((B247 - M20)/5,0), where B247 contains the Future value; the factor 5 is adjusted for each of the Future Options and is the difference between strike prices for that particular Future Options. For example, for the grain futures the factor is 10, for oil the factor is 50, for the Treasury Futures the factor is one. For Yen Futures the factor is 5, but the multiplier factor is 1,000, so the equation for computing the Yen Long Call or Put is: = IF($G263 > 80,5 * ROUND(1,000 * $B263/5,0),"")

Long Put = M22 - 5, where M22 contains the strike price of the Short Put and 5 is the next lower Put strike price. *Note:* for Future options that have strike prices closer spaced than 5 points, the 5 would be adjusted accordingly, for example 1 for US Bonds and US 10 Year Notes while the Corn future Options have strike prices 10 apart.

Note: the same information and equations are included in the spreadsheets for the 10 Future Options listed above.

The Columns H and I in the spreadsheets are for signaling when WWI has triggered a potentially profitable Debit Spread position. The Column J can be used for computing the cost of opening the Debit Spread and Column K can be used for computing the short-term profit (or loss) of these short-term positions which are normally open for a few trading days.

The Capital Growth sheet with the software shows a period from Oct 03 to Oct 08 or a period of five years. Assuming no losses and the number of options increased each six months as five, this model shows with a beginning capital of $25,000. At the end of five years your capital would have grown to $981,784.

The Capital Growth sheet has extrapolated capital values based on the simplistic model described above. You should enter the actual trades results each month to give you your actual capital growth. The model will extrapolate your predicted capital growth. So the sheet has a dual purpose: (1) provide you with a record of your trades and (2) provide you a prediction of your capital growth using your actual initial capital. In the "increase in number of options" in cell B2 you may enter a number greater than or less than the current 5 to suit your own trading style.

How to Use the Common Format Spreadsheets

The common format was shown above. Each day you should enter the closing market values of the futures: KWheat, corn, soybeans, coffee, oil, SPX Futures, USBonds, US 10yr Notes, and Yen Futures for today's date on their respective spreadsheets. The sheets have a unique feature that extrapolates the future market value for each sheet for its commodity or future. This extrapolation is based on the previous 20 days using the following equation: = SUM(B232:B251)/20, where B232:B251 are the market values over those 20 days and SUM is the Excel function for summing values over a range of cells; by dividing this sum by 20 it computes the average value for the last 20 days to provide the estimated value. I find this a handy guide to tell me where the market is headed during the remainder of the Option Month, since each market chart shows the value of the underlying future to the next expiration date.

An example of the KWheat chart is presented in the SelfAdapFutOp software. In this chart the extrapolation begins about 24 Sep 03, where the KWheat curve becomes smooth covered by the 20-day moving average (smooth curve).

At the beginning of the Option Month, you can open a 2 sigma Corn Covered Credit Spread, the strategy provided corn has an expiration during the new Option Month. Your objective is to open a Call credit spread and a Put credit spread obtaining the greatest initial credit possible. It is *not* necessary to open both the Call and Put sides of the credit spread at the same time or even on the same day. Here is a tip to increase your monthly profit: check the 2 sig Corn Call and Put Short Strike Prices and the Long Call Strike Prices, and check from your market data website for the new month's premiums for the four strike prices and insert these values in the Call and Put equations that calculate the Initial Credit that would be received. Rather than use these premiums for the order you place with your website broker increase the value by 0.1 or 0.2 more than is quoted. This way the daily volatility and the increased volatility at the beginning of a new Option Month will help you obtain more initial credit and therefore more profit at the expiration of the new Option Month. The equations for the initial credit were presented on the fourth page of this chapter. The **margin** for 15 Corn 2 sig covered credit spreads = 10 * 15 * 50 * 2 = **$15,000.** I recommend you have double the margin amount in your account to open a credit spread. I believe corn is the best of the Future options for covered credit spreads.

Targets of Opportunity: WWI > 80 or WWI < 20

You should scan your 10 market spreadsheets daily seeking the WWI triggers which are indicated in Column H for WWI < 20 triggering a potential profitable Call Debit Spread or Long Call. If you decide to open such a position, the Long Call would be at-the-money, or the Call strike prices closest to the market.

An example: In scanning the sheets on 11 Sep 03, the KWheat sheet showed a WWI = 7.15, badly oversold and cell H241 showed a value 40, indicating a KWheat Debit Spread Oct C40/C50 would be a potentially profitable position to open. A position was opened by buying 10 KWheat Oct Long Call 40 Short C50 for a cost = $3,063, computed by the equation: = 10 * 50 * (14.375 - 8.25), where 10 is the number of options, 6.125 is the premium difference, and 50 is the $/point for KWheat Future options. Oct options were used because Dec expiration options would have been more costly. Four trading days later on 17 Sep 03 the WWI = 52 signaling that the market had risen as predicted by the WWI < 20 and the Call Debit Spread should be closed to take the profit which was small, only $63. This was not very profitable, but some trades are more profitable. WWI triggers allow you to add to your monthly profit.

Trading Results for 10 Future Options – WWI Triggered

The 10 Futures options were tracked for over a year. The WWI-triggered trades were indicated using the equations:

1. For Call Debit Spreads = IF($G256 < 20,10 * ROUND($B256/10,0),"")
2. For Put Debit Spreads = IF($G256 > 80,10 * ROUND($B256/10,0),""))

In this evaluation of the Debit Spread strategy, the trade for a Call Debit Spread was triggered when WWI < 20 and for a Put Debit Spread when WWI > 80. The biggest problem in using this strategy is the condition of *hang up* when the WWI remains > 80 for many days or the condition of *stick down* when the WWI stays below 20 for many days. These conditions are combated for most of the future options by using the tactic of *triads*, which means the triggered position was opened for *three days.* Then the position would be closed with a profit or loss. This triad (three days) tactic was a method for limiting losses if the market was not moving as rapidly as we wanted in the direction predicted by the WWI. Remember, when the WWI > 80, this means the market is predicting a drop soon; when WWI < 20 the market is predicting a rise promptly. In the case of the US Bond Future Options and the US 10Year Note Future Options, then a *duad or a two-day limit loss tactic was used* because of the higher cost amounts involved for these two future options.

The Gold, Corn, and Kansas City Wheat Future Options were the best profit makers in that order, all receiving A+ or A ratings. The A rankings had an Average Profit per Trade relative to cost return of 35% or more. The A + ranking had a return greater than 45%. Gold was the best with a profit of $5,560, only seven trades, for an average profit per trade of $794.

SUMMARY OF SELADAPTFUTOP.XLS

The SelfAdaptiveFutOp Software (Excel Workbook) by Jon Schiller provides you with an excellent method for generating a steady monthly income using the **2 sigma SPX Covered Credit Spread** strategy and augmenting the monthly income with targets of opportunity using the WWI-triggered Debit Spreads or Long positions of Future Option. Remember: (1) WWI > 80 triggers a Put Debit Spread. (2) WWI < 20 triggers a Call Debit Spread. Note: Corn Future Options were also found to yield profitable 2 sigma Credit Covered Spreads.

SELF-ADAPTIVE CURRENCY TRADING SOFTWARE: SELFADAPCUR.XLS

This software package show strategies for trading the world's largest currencies/$ triggered by the Welles-Wilder Indicator (WWI). Each data sheet of the software has the capability of making the computations for the WWI so you can use it as an indicator of when to Buy or Sell the Currency.

A quick review of the strategies:

Buy the Currency when it is triggered by WWI < 20: Buy the currency and hold for a few days until selling the currency can make a profit. A profit will result when the position is sold, unless the WWI stays less than 20 for many days (*the stuck-down condition*) that could cause a loss.

Sell the Currency when it is triggered by WWI > 80: Sell the currency and hold for a few days until buying the currency can make a profit. A profit will result when the position is bought back, unless the WWI stays greater than 80 for many days (*the hung-up condition)* which could cause a loss.

This Software has a sheet for each of the following currencies relative to the US$:

1. Euro/$ A Lot of Euro = 100,000
2. Swiss Franc/$ A Lot of SFranc = 125,000
3. Yen/$ A Lot of Yen = 15,000,000
4. UK Lb/$ A Lot of UK Lb = 75,000
5. Yen-Euro Hedge/$ Buy a Lot of Euro and Sell a Lot of Yen for one Hedge Position

In addition to these five sheets there are five charts with the Currency or the Hedge and the WWI plus two special sheets called CapitalGrowth and CapGrwthChart. The Capital Growth sheet can be used for keeping track of your actual profit and losses to show your actual capital in dollars. This sheet uses a simplistic model based on the WWI-triggered Currency positions. The extrapolation assumes you begin with $4,000 initial capital and use 1 Lot of Currency for the WWI-triggered Buy or Sells. The algorithms will adjust the number of Lots based on your initial capital and will show the resulting capital growth. The numbers of Lots are increased by one each quarter of the year. You may adjust this increase in number of Lots for more aggressive trading or decrease the number of lots for more conservative trading.

After the CapGrwthChart is a sheet called CurrentMktData for entering the current day's market for the four currencies (the Euro, SFranc, Yen,and UKLB). You may use this sheet for entering the realtime end-of-day market data from the Internet using mgforex.com, or some other market data web page. You may enter the value into the row of today's date in Column B which contains the market data by copying the market value and then *paste special value* in the cell B248 for the date of 22 Sep 03. The cells are the same in all currency spreadsheets, which makes using the software easier for the user.

COMMON FORMAT FOR THE 4 CURRENCY EXCEL SPREADSHEETS

A B C D E F G H I J K L M N

Column A has the date in the format: 25 Sep 03

Column B has the underlying market name, for example Euro, SFranc, Yen, UKLB.

Column C computes the market movement up using the equation: = IF((B7 - B6) > 0,B7 - B6,0)

Column D computes the market movement down using the equation: = IF((B7 - B6) < 0,B7 - B6,0)

Column E computes the Up 7-day exponential moving average using the equation: = E6 * 0.75 + C7 * 0.25

Column F computes the Down 7-day exponential moving average using the equation: = F6 * 0.75 + D7 * 0.25

Column G computes the Welles-Wilder Indicator using the equation: = 100 * (E7/(E7 - F7))

Column H contains the number of Currency Lots set to 1; the value of the Lot in currency/$ in cell H1, for Euro H1 = 100,000/$, for SFranc H1= 125,000/ $, for Yen H1 = 15,000,000/$, for UKLB H1= 75,000/$

Column I computes if the WWI < 20 using the equation: = IF($G7 < 20,5 * ROUND($B7/5,0),"")

Column J computes if the WWI > 80 using the equation: = IF($G7 > 80,5 * ROUND($B7/5,0),"")

Column K computes the triggered Currency trade using the equation: = H239 * $H$1/B239

Column L computes the profit for the trade using the equation: = K246 - K239, where K246 contains the value of selling 1 Lot of the currency to close the Lot previously bought and K239 is the value of buying 1 Lot of currency which in this example WWI had triggered a Buy (WWI < 20) seven trading days earlier. *Note:* in this example for Euro/$ currency the profit for the seven days was $2,505 which had required a Margin of $1,000.

Column M computes the cumulative profit for the trades from 17 Oct 02 to the present.

Column N computes the average profit/month. For the Euro the average profit/mo was $1,672 for the 11 months from 17 Oct 02 through 18 Sep 03.

Notes:

1. The row numbers 6 and 7 depend on the row number of the date for the day of the computation
2. The values depend on the underlying market value in Column B, Row 7 for the date of 18 Oct 02 for the above spreadsheet example.
3. The dates in the spreadsheets begin with 17 Oct 02 which is row 6, the first date for which there is data for the currencies.
4. In order to simplify the date algorithm, holidays are included if they fall on Mon through Fri and the market value in Column B is set equal to the previous market value.

The 2 Standard Deviation Computation is a measure of the currency volatility. Standard Deviation (sig) is computed using Excel's STDEV function using the last 10 months in the spreadsheet segment which goes from cell O1 to Q20. This information is for the Euro currency, but similar tables are included in the spreadsheets for the other currencies: the Swiss Franc, the British Pound, and the Yen.

The Capital Growth sheet included in this software shows a period from Oct 03 to Oct 08 (5 years). Assuming no losses and assuming the number of options increased each six months as five, this model shows that, with a beginning capital of $4,000, at the end of five years your capital would have grown to $1,117,707.

The CapitalGrowth sheet has extrapolated capital values based on the simplistic model described above. You should enter the actual trades results each month to give you your actual capital growth. The model will extrapolate your predicted capital growth. So the sheet has a dual purpose: (1) provide you with a record of your trades and (2) provide you a prediction of your capital growth using your actual initial capital. In the "increase in number of Options" in cell B2 you may enter a number greater than or less than the current five to suit your own trading style.

How to Use the Common Format Spreadsheets

The common format was shown above. Each day you should enter the closing market values of the Euro, SFranc, Yen, and UKLB for today's date on their respective spreadsheets. The sheets have a unique feature that extrapolates the future market value for each sheet for it's respective currencies. This extrapolation is based on the previous 20 days using the following equation: =SUM(B232:B251)/20, where B232:B251 are the market values over those 20 days and SUM is the Excel function for summing values over a range of cells; by dividing this sum by 20 it computes the average value for the last 20 days to provide the estimated value. I find this a handy guide to tell me where the market is headed during the remainder of the Option Month, since each market chart shows the value of the underlying currency to the next options expiration date (the options expiration dates are used so that if you are doing both currency and options trading you have a common date base to use).

Targets of Opportunity: WWI > 80 or WWI < 20

You should scan your four currency spreadsheets daily seeking the WWI triggers which are indicated in the Columns H for WWI < 20 triggering a potential profitable Buy currency Lot. If you decide to Buy 1 (or more) Lot, the Buy order should be given to your internet broker. I recommend considering the currency broker at mgforex.com, which permits an account to be open for one month of free paper trading. It has low commission rates and appears to be a good broker.

An example: In scanning the sheets on Tu 9 Sep 03, the Euro sheet showed a WWI = 16.88, indicating a Buy of 1 Lot of Euros would be a potentially profitable position to open. A position was opened by buying 1 Lot for a cost = $109,842, computed by the equation: = H232 * $H$1/B232, where H232 is the number of Lots (1). $H$1 is 100,000 the number of Euros in one Lot. B232 was the value of Euro, $112,347, meaning that if the 1 Lot of Euros were sold to close the position, then a seven-day profit of $2,505 would result. *This example is typical and shows the potential power of the WWI-triggered Buy or Sell of currency Lots.* WWI-triggered positions can be used for all four of the currencies.

A brief summary of the Yen-Euro hedge strategy will be given here: the hedge is buying Euros and selling Yen for one side of the hedge. When WWI < 20, then buy the hedge. Close when a profit is made. When WWI > 80, then sell the hedge. Close when a profit is made.

Summary of SelfAdapCur.xls Software

The SelfAdaptiveCurrTrd Software (Excel Workbook) by Jon Schiller provides you with an excellent method for generating good profits. The table below shows the average profit per month achieved during the year of paper trades for the four currencies and the Yen-Euro hedge at the trading level of 1 Lot:

Euro	SFranc	Yen	UKLB	Yen-Euro Hedge
\$1,672	\$638	\$1,195	\$1,153	\$1,511

As may be seen by the table above the Euro had the best monthly average profit at \$1,672/mo and the Yen-Euro Hedge had the second best at \$1,511/mo.

The WWI-triggered Buying and Selling has the potential of high profits for low Margin. Remember: (1) WWI < 20 triggers a Buy one or more Lots. (2) WWI > 80 triggers a Sell one or more Lots. After a Buy or Sell, the position should be closed after a profit which typically takes seven trading days. The required Margin for one Lot is \$1,000; however I recommend a minimum account size of \$4,000 to trade one Lot. *Note:* for the Hedge trading when WWI < 20 then Buy the hedge and after a profit occurs, then close. When the WWI > 80 sell the hedge and when a profit is generated, then close.

Self-Adaptive Stock Trading Software: SelfAdapStockTrading

This is a description of the software for the nine common stocks included in the Software SelfAdaptiveStockTrading. This software uses two basic strategies:

1. Buying or Selling the Stocks triggered by the Welles-Wilder Indicator (WWI).
2. Buying the Stocks for a Year and Holding. Sell to Collect Profit

Each sheet of the software has the computations for the 2 sigma, the computations for the WWI and an indication of whether a Buy of Sell the Stock.

A quick review of the strategies:

Buy Stocks triggered when WWI < 20: Buy Stocks near close of day when trigger occurs. Sell Stocks a few days later to close position when a Profit occurs if the market rises as the WWI predicts it will, then a profit will result when the Stock is Sold. If the WWI ***sticks down < 20*** for three days without a profit, close the position by selling the stock and take a small loss.

Sell Stocks triggered when WWI > 80: Sell Stocks near close of day when trigger occurs as a ***short sell***. Buy Stocks a few days later when a Profit occurs if the market drops as the WWI predicts it will, then a profit will result when the Stock is bought back to close the Short Position. If the WWI hangs up > 80 for three days without a profit, close the position by buying the stock back to close the short position and take a small loss.

Buy the Stocks for a Year and Hold: This is a very simple strategy. The Stock is purchased, it is assumed that 200 Shares are purchased, and any splits that occur will double your shares to 400 as happened in two of the stocks included in this software (eBay and Microsoft). After a year you can sell and take your profit, or hold and continue making your stock equity grow. *The stocks included in this software are among the top performing stocks in terms of equity growth.*

This Software has a Sheet for calculating trading parameters and a Chart for each of the following Stocks:

1. Amgen Stocks
2. Cisco Stocks
3. Dell Stocks
4. eBay Stocks
5. Intel Stocks
6. IBM Stocks
7. Microsoft (Msft) Stocks
8. Nasd100Tr (QQQQ) Stocks
9. Oracle Stocks
10. Yahoo Stocks

In addition to these 10 sheets and 10 charts, a special sheet called CapitalGrowth and CapGrwthChart is provided to aid you in extrapolating your expected profits through Jan 09 or some five years into the future. The Capital Growth sheet can be used for keeping track of your actual profit and losses to show your actual capital in dollars. This sheet uses a simplistic model based on the buying or selling blocks of stocks from among the 10 common stocks when triggered by the WWI. The extrapolation assumes you begin with $25,000 initial capital and you buy or sell blocks of 200 stocks. The algorithms will adjust the number of blocks based on your initial capital, when you enter your actual beginning Capital into cell K2 of the CapitalGrowth sheet, and the capital growth computations will be adjusted accordingly. You could begin with less capital, but I recommend you begin with at least $25,000 (and you will get better attention from your broker with that starting amount). The number of blocks are increased in July and January of each year. You may adjust this increase number for more aggressive trading or make it less for more conservative trading.

After the CapGrwthChart is a sheet called CurrentMktData for entering the current day's market data for the 10 stocks. You may use this sheet for entering the realtime end-of-day market data from the Internet using Interquote, or some other market data web page. You may link the value into the row of today's date in Column B which contains the market data by copying the market value and then *PASTE SPECIAL, VALUE* in the cell B248 for the data for 22 September 03. The cells are the same in all 10 Stock spreadsheets, which makes using the software easier for the user.

Common Format for the 11 Excel Spreadsheets

A B C D E F G H I J K L M N O P

Column A has the trading date in the format 6 May 06.

Column B has the underlying market name, for example Amgen, Cisco, Dell, eBay, etc.

Column C computes the market movement up using the equation: = IF((B7 - B6) > 0,B7 - B6,0)

Column D computes the market movement down using the equation: = IF((B7 - B6) < 0,B7 - B6,0)

Column E computes the Up 7-day exponential moving average using the equation: = E6 * 0.75 + C7 * 0.25

Column F computes the Down 7-day exponential moving average using the equation: = F6 * 0.75 + D7 * 0.25

Column G computes the Welles-Wilder Indicator using the equation: = 100 * (E7/(E7 - F7))

Column H computes if the WWI < 20 using the equation: = IF($G246 < 20,B246,"")

Column I computes if the WWI > 80 using the equation: = IF($G245 > 80,B245,"")

Notes:

1. The row numbers 6 and 7 depend on the row number of the date for the day of the computation
2. The values depend on the underlying market value in Column B, Row 7 for the date of 18 Oct 02 for the above spreadsheet example.
3. The dates in the spreadsheets begin with 17 Oct 02 which is row 6, the first date for which there is data for the OEX and the nine stocks.
4. In order to simplify the date algorithm, holidays are included if they fall on Monday through Friday and the market value in Column B is set equal to the previous market value.

Column J shows the value of the action: a cost if the stock is bought, or a credit if the stock is sold.

Column K computes the profit (or loss) of the several-day action.

Column L computes the cumulative profit (or loss) to date.

Column M computes the average Profit (or loss) per month.

Here the Spreadsheet SWITCHES to the EQUITY INCREASE STRATEGY

Column N computes the daily value of the original 200 Shares of Stock Purchased. If the stocks doubles by a split, then the number of shares would be increased to 400 shares, as happened for eBay and Microsoft.

Column O computes the daily Equity Profit or Increase in value of year to date.

Column P is the last Column of the Spreadsheet and computes the year-to-date %Equity Increase of the stock in the spreadsheet. There are nine identical formatted spreadsheets, which differ only by the individual stock's daily data from 17 Oct 02 up to the current date. As those of you who have used my software before know, I extrapolate using a 20-day extrapolation equation as follows: = SUM(B249:B268)/20. This extrapolation allows you to project 20 days ahead, where the stock value is likely to move.

Summary of Results of Strategy 1: WWI-Triggered Buying/Selling

As may be seen, Intel, eBay and Microsoft were clear winners with A+ ratings for using with this strategy. Cisco is the only one that received an F since it lost money. Dell received a C- rating with only $82 profit and Oracle got a D since it only made $17 for the year. Yahoo was not included in this contest.

If you're going to trade this strategy, I presume you would only use the A+ performers which had an annual return of 38% and an average monthly income $424.

Summary of Results of Strategy 2: Buy 200 Shares & Hold for 1 Yr.

The software picks out nine good stocks to use for **buying and holding.** All stocks but one did better to buy and hold than to trade triggered by WWI.

As you may see, all stocks rate in the A range except Dell, Oracle and Microsoft. eBay is clearly the winner in this one year Equity Race! Also Yahoo was not ranked in this contest.

How Do the Two Strategies Compare Side by Side?

eBay was best using either strategy. Strategy 2 was almost twice as profitable as Strategy 1.

How to Use the Common Format Spreadsheets

The common format was shown above. Each day you should enter the closing market values of the Amgen, Cisco, Dell, eBay, IBM, Intel, Msft, QQQQ, and Oracle for today's date on their respective spreadsheets. The sheets have a unique feature that extrapolates the future market value for each sheet for its respective stock. This extrapolation is based on the previous 20 days using the following equation: = SUM(B232:B251)/20, where B232:B251 are the market values over those 20 days and SUM is the Excel function for summing values over a range of cells; by dividing this sum by 20 it computes the average value for the last 20 days to provide the estimated value. I find this a handy guide to tell me where the market is headed during the remainder of the month, since each market chart shows the value of the underlying stock or OEX to the next expiration date.

Following are the one year Charts for each of these nine stocks. *I find these charts useful with the 50-day trendline included since the big Fund Managers seem to use this as a guide for buying and selling a particular stock.* These charts are generated in the Bonus Software Package *SelfAdapStockTrading.*

How to Get Started with Strategy 2 – the Most Profitable Way

Since eBay was the most profitable for the last year, it will probably be profitable for the upcoming year. Two hundred shares would cost about $10,000, so using my rule of double the capital in your account, to open the 200 eBay longs, you should have a total capital = **$20,000** in your account.

Targets of Opportunity for Strategy 1: WWI > 80 or WWI < 20

You should scan your 10 market spreadsheets daily seeking the WWI triggers which are indicated in the Columns H for WWI < 20, triggering a potential profitable Long or Short position. If you decide to open such a position, you would place an order to buy at a realtime value or a few hundredths of a point to your favor to make your website broker work for his money. I have assumed you would use a low commission broker such as Ameritrade who advertises in IBD to charge $10.99 per trade no matter how many shares. So in the computations in the software I used $22 per round trip trade for commission costs.

An example: in scanning the spreadsheets on Thursday 18 September 03, the day before September options expiration, the Dell sheet showed WWI = 80.94 and cell I246 showed a value for Dell at strike price 35 indicating a 200 share block sold short would be a credit = $6,988. This was computed by the equation: = 200 * B246, where 200 is the number of shares sold short. Two trading days later, on Monday 22 September 03 the WWI = 40.46, signaling that the market had dropped as predicted and the WWI and the short position should be closed by placing an order to buy back the October Dell block at 34.08 for a cost of $6,816 including the round-trip commission cost of $22. This two-trading-day transaction yielded a profit = $150 or a return on investment = 2.12%. This example is typical and shows the potential power of the WWI-triggered long positions for stocks.

Summary

The SelfAdapStockTrading.xls Software (Excel Workbook) by Jon Schiller provides you with an excellent method for generating a steady monthly income using **Strategy 1 or Strategy 2**. Remember: (1) WWI > 80 triggers a Sell 200 Shares Short or when WWI < 20 triggers a Buy 200 Shares. (2) a simple short time investment.

I recommend you do *paper* trading for a month or two using the software, keeping it updated daily and making the *paper* trades, getting a feel for how the strategies work in practice. After you feel confident, then you can switch to real trading. The author is available at email address jonsch1@verizon.net to answer any questions about the functioning of the software. *Please do not ask for trading advice, that is beyond the scope of my help!*

I have now a new website, where I keep the new items I have to offer to the Options and Currency trader in the way of books and software.
www.jonschilleroptions.com/Home1.html

An excellent near-realtime futures, futures options and futures broker is on website: www.orionfutures.com. By clicking on Quotes, you obtain all the listed Futures in Chapter 6. After obtaining a Futures quote, you may obtain the Futures Options by clicking on Options Prices. The futures market closes a half hour before the NYSE closing.

Appendix A

Some Websites to Aid Options & Currency Trading

Interquote: **www.interquote.com**, for realtime index option and stock options, has a small monthly subscription fee. Uses the options exchange letter codes for months and strike prices.

The Website for Currency Trading: **www.mgforex.com** permits one month of free *paper trading* to become aware of the realities of Currency Trading.

Near-realtime Options Quotations: **www.cbs.com** is a free service with quotes about five minutes delayed. Uses the options exchange letter codes for months and strike prices.

Near Realtime Futures Quotations: **www.futexch.com** provides a wide range of futures quotations with attractive format.

If you don't have the exact spelling for a website, then enter the spelling you believe is correct into Google search; you will obtain the possible websites to access. For example, if you enter "Currency Brokers" in Google search, you will obtain over a dozen possible brokers and websites with currency trading information.

MORE WEBSITES TO AID YOUR TRADING:

www.Optionsxpress.com: This is a website broker that has a section called Options 101 that summarizes basic options principles.
www.CBS.marketwatch.com: This website is a good place to receive near realtime options data based on a user portfolio of the data you wish.
www.cnn.com: This website is a widely used website for obtaining CNN type financial data.
www.Finance.yahoo.com: One of the widest used financial websites with 8.9 million users.
www.Moneycentral.msn.com: The top-used financial website in mid 2003 with 9.2 million users.
www.fool.com: A website used for all types of good financial information.
www.Forbes.com: A Forbes magazine website with good financial data.
www.Fortune.com: A website of the famous magazine Fortune.
www.Businessweek.com: Another widely read magazine website.
www.Bizjournals.com: Another widely used financial website.
www.Bankrate.com: The fifth most-used investment data website.
www.Investors.com: Investment Business Day (IBD) website for those interested in high-growth stock purchases. Special features are provided for IBD subscribers.
www.Investinginbonds.com: Has the basics of bond investing, market statistics and retirement planning ideas.
www.Precision-info.com: Sponsored by Ameritrade with advice on investment strategies.
www.Zacks.com: Research and analytical tools for investors with financial information
www.Sec.gov: An official website for the Securities and Exchange commission whose mission is to protect investors and protect security markets from wrongdoing.
www.Schaeffersresearch.com: A website that features Puts and Calls Options. Uses so-called "contrarian" theory applied to stocks with technical trends contrary to current investor expectations.
www.Briefing.com: A website of overall business information helpful to the active online trader.
www.Thestreet.com: An individual guide to Wall Street to provide news, investment tools and commentary.
www.Firstcall.com: A website operated by Thompson Corp. which provides

weekly market commentary with data on what market affecting announcements have been made and a diary of market announcements coming during the remainder of the week.
www.Investopedia.com: An Investment encyclopedia defining financial terms.

A further list of financial websites to consider:
www.Wallstreetcity.com
www.Marktwise.com
www.Traderbot.com
www.Advancedanalyzer.com
www.Marketedge.com

Remember my favorite realtime portfolio-based website for all types of Options, Puts and Calls, including the underlying market figures: **www.Interquote.com**

Appendix B

Some Website Brokers

B&J for Index & Stock Options Trades: **www.bandjtrading.com**
A reliable, low-cost broker who specializes in index and stock options. I have used B&J for over 20 years. Has an easy-to-use website for entering complex orders such as spreads, orders and the open orders and confirmation when the orders have been filled. Has reliable back-up phone service with good brokers. Typical Broker Commission for 15 Call & Put Covered Credit Spreads = $204, including all fees.

Currency Trades: **www.mgforex.com**
Recommended by a veteran currency trader from Madrid. Has an easy-to-use website for entering e-currency orders.

Future Options Trades: **www.orionfutures.com**
A low-cost website broker who specializes in Future Options. Provides easy-to-use quotes for all Futures and Future Options. Does not provide service for Index or Stock Options.

Stock and Options Trading: **www.ameritrade.com**
A very low-cost website broker who charges $22 round-trip broker commission no matter how many stocks or options traded. I used their commission cost in the Chapter 8 Stock Trading examples. They proudly advertise no special order handling fees and market orders and limit orders have same one-way commission $10.99.

APPENDIX C

ANSWERS TO TEST QUESTIONS

1. OEX Options code Test from Chapter I
    1) March Call 620
    2) November Put 525
    3) May Put 385
    4) March Put 595
    5) January Call 680

2. Currency Test in Chapter I
    1) 3 * 100,000/0.8123 = $369,322,
    2) 3 * 1,000 = $3,000
    3) 2 * 1,000 = $2,000
    4) 5 * 15,000,000/117.90 Yen/$
    5) 2 * 1,000 = $2,000

APPENDIX D

COMPARISON OF MARKET INDICATORS AS TRIGGERS

WWI vs STOCHASTICS%K -%D

Stochastics%K - %D was the most complex market indicator covered in Chapter 9, the survey of market indicators. There is good correlation between the two market indicators Stoch%K-%D and WWI. A Plot showed that when Stochastics > 0, then WWI > 50 and when Stochastics < 0 the WWI < 50.

WWI vs MAD9-4

MAD9-4 indicator was a fairly simple market indicator covered in Chapter 9, the survey of market indicators. The indicator takes the difference between the four-day exponential moving average and the nine-day exponential moving average. Comparing the MAD9-4 indicator and WWI for the OEX shows close correlation shows that with the WWI > 45 corresponding to the MAD9-4 > 0.

WWI vs MAD4

The comparison between the MAD4 and the WWI shows that there is good correlation between the two indicators:

1. when MAD4 > 0, then WWI > 60
2. when MAD4 < 0, WWI < 40.

WWI vs MADC

MADC indicator was a relatively complex market indicator covered in Chapter 9, the survey of market indicators. In comparing the MADC indicator and WWI for the OEX on the shows a very close correlation between the fluctuations of the MADC and the WWI. When the WWI is greater than 50, the MADC is positive; when the WWI is less than 50 the MADC is negative.

WWI vs BOLLINGER BAND

The Bollinger Band chart is a good competitor to the WWI two-level market indicator. A value of the market indicator above the upper band is overbought, analogous to the WWI > 80. A value of the market indicator below the lower band is oversold, analogous to the WWI < 20. One may compare charts compares the Upper and Lower Bollinger Bands with the WWI for the OEX on the same plot by using the Yahoo website: http://finance.yahoo.com/ By clicking on OEX, then selecting TECHNICAL ANALYSIS, next clicking on BOLLINGER BAND and then RSI (which is WWI}. My comparison of these two indicators shows that WWI is more sensitive than BBI in telling when the OEX is *overbought* or *oversold* as a trigger for trading the Debit Spreads.

SUMMARY

We have compared the WWI with the Up and Down market Indicators: the Stochastics%K - %D, the MADC, the MAD9-4, and the MAD4 correlate closely with the WWI fluctuations. Generally when the Up and Down indicator is positive, then the WWI is greater than 50. When the Up and Down indicator is negative, then the WWI is less than 50.

The WWI was then compared with the Bollinger Band Indicator which is another indicator for showing when the underlying market is overbought or oversold. This comparison was made to show how the two indicators correlated in showing the overbought and oversold conditions. The correlation was good, but the WWI was more sensitive in showing shifts in direction that can be used for trading. In other words, the strategy of this book that shows the WWI as an effective trigger for Call Debit Spreads or Put Debit Spreads or when to Buy or Sell Currencies is on the right track. The hazard of Hang-up or Stick-down of the WWI was even worse for the Bollinger Band Indicator.

Appendix E

Daily & Monthly Tasks

This appendix will present the tasks you, the trader, must perform on a periodic basis in the format of the Microsoft Excel program (part of Microsoft Office). These tasks are performed on the SelfAdaptive Software Packets or whatever spreadsheet program, such as Sun Microsystems' StarOffice 7 or Corel's WordPerfect Office 11, you may use. I have used Corel's spreadsheet program and it is very similar to Excel. For example, it has a standard deviation function, but it is called something different than STDEV. I have provided you with all the equations so you may create your own spreadsheet software and charts.

Update Market Values in Spreadsheets Daily

Each day you must enter the closing values of all the market signals you are tracking: the OEX and the 11 Stocks, the 10 Futures used for the Futures Options, and the 4 Currencies and 1 currency hedge.

Scan Spreadsheets Daily for WWI Triggers Daily

After entering the daily market values, you should scan each spreadsheet to find any WWI triggers for Call Debit Spreads, Put Debit Spreads, or Currency Buy or Sell signals. If you find a trigger, you must then decide whether to place an order as signaled by the WWI being greater than 80 or less than 20. You should also check to make sure neither your Short Call or Short Put of any open credit spreads is being threatened by a penetration or near penetration. You must decide on any corrective action should there be a threat to a Short.

Open New Covered Credit Spreads Monthly

One of your most important tasks, and the one I find the most fun, is to open the new 2sig Covered Credit Spreads. This will give you the sense of generating your monthly income. Fortunately your spreadsheet which computes the 2 sigma values as well as the Short and Long Calls and Puts takes care of most of the work automatically when you enter the latest market data. Then you must go to the section of your spreadsheet where these computations are made and determine your order parameters.

Once you have decided to make the order and the parameters: number of options, Call Strike Prices, Put Strike Prices and the premium differences you are asking, you open Internet and enter your order on your broker's website order entry section. Then you should check the broker's website a few times during the day until the order is confirmed as filled. If you asked for too much and the order is not filled on either the Call or Put side, then you should try again for the next day, now armed with the closing prices for the unsuccessful day. *Remember my Hint to ask for 0.1 or 0.2 more than the quoted premium difference, this allowing the daily volatility to increase your Initial Credit.*

APPENDIX F

THEORY OF CAPITAL SHIFTS FOR BIG MARKET MOVEMENTS

I have noted that when there is a large jump in the market such as Mon, 3 Nov 03, when the OEX jumped 4.03, the Gold Futures dropped by 7.03, an unusually large drop. In addition, US Bond Futures dropped 18/32 and US 10-Year Note Futures dropped 16.5/32. It appears that large traders sold their Gold, US Bond and 10-Year note futures in order to obtain cash to buy stocks in the NY stock markets. The following table attempts to validate this theory. This theory was validated for 60% of the cases examined.

THEORY: When OEX Jumps, Gold & US Bond Futures Drop						
Date	OEX	OEX delta	Gold Fut	Gold F Cnge	US Bnd Fut	US Bnd F Cnge
18-Sep-03	522.6	7.17	376.6	0.4	110.0625	0.0625
29-Sep-03	505.02	5.41	382.4	1.6	110.34375	-0.78125
1-Oct-03	510.33	11.77	384.3	-1.1	111.3125	-0.84375
28-Oct-03	518.64	7.87	383.2	-4.7	109.5625	0.78125
3-Nov-03	524.01	4.03	377	-7.5	108.15625	-0.5625
			Validation	60.00%		60.00%

Printed in the United States
76181LV00003B/97